CW01367900

THE CRAFTSMAN IN THE CITY

Clothworkers' Hall Refurbished

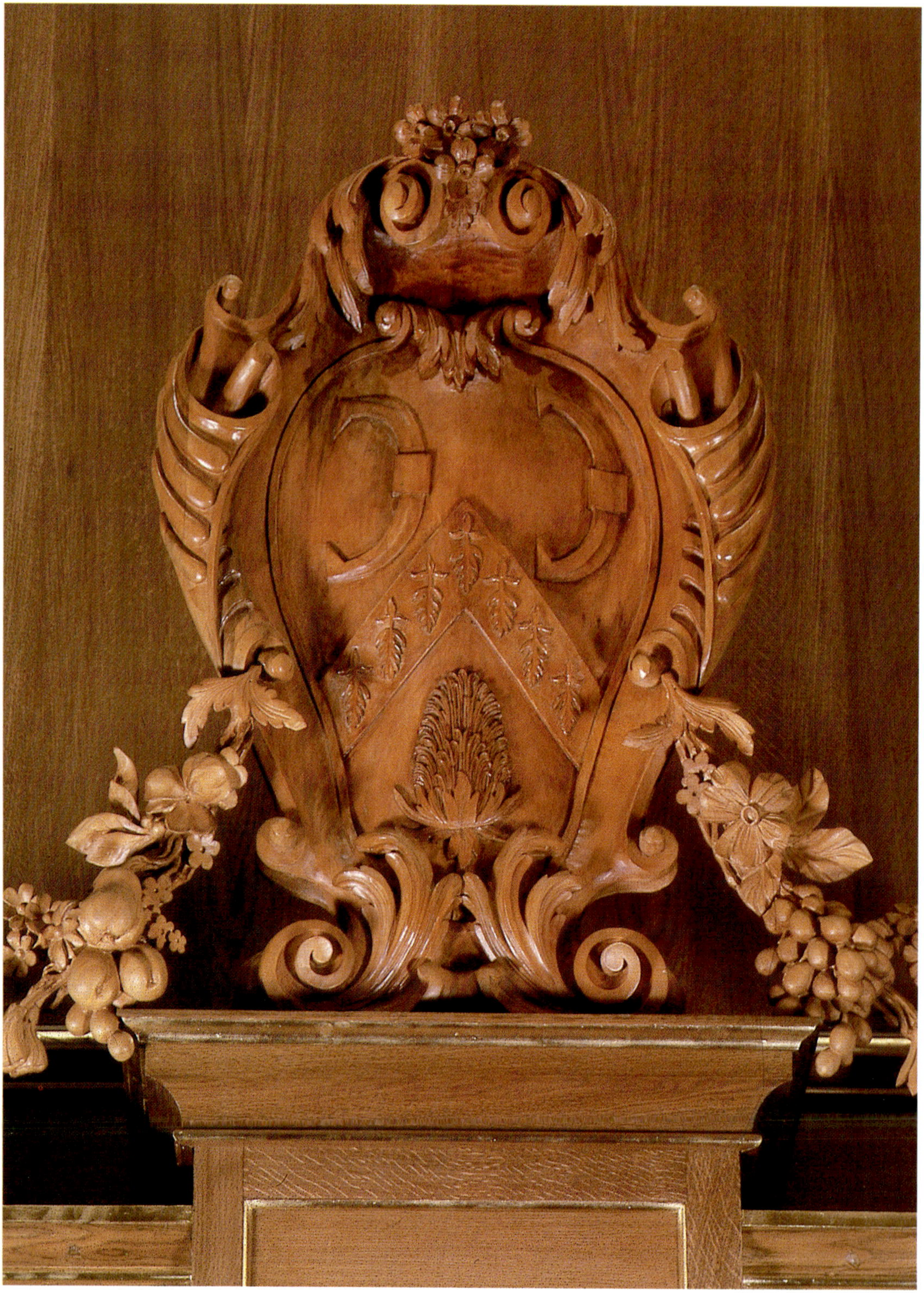

THE CRAFTSMAN IN THE CITY

Clothworkers' Hall Refurbished

NICHOLAS THOMPSON, B.Arch., RIBA
Donald W. Insall and Associates Ltd.

Published by Diptych, London
in association with The Clothworkers' Company

Published by Diptych
11 Bettridge Road
London SW6 3QH

Copyright © The Clothworkers' Company

First published in 1987

All rights reserved. No part of this publication
may be reproduced, stored in any retrieval system,
or transmitted in any form or by any means,
electronic, mechanical, photocopying or otherwise
without the prior permission in writing of
the Publisher.

ISBN 1 870627 01 6

Typeset and printed by BAS Printers Limited, Over Wallop
and bound by Hunter and Foulis, Edinburgh.

Cover design: Langley Iddins

Frontispiece: The coat of arms of The Clothworkers'
Company: a cartouche carved in lime wood for
the Livery Hall by Anthony Harrington.

Illustrations for this book have been provided by
The Clothworkers' Company, Higgs and Hill PLC,
Cresswell Photographic Studios Ltd and Donald W. Insall
and Associates Ltd. The coloured drawing on page 19 is
reproduced by permission of The Guildhall Library.

Publishers Acknowledgement
My thanks are particularly due to
Mr. David Wickham and Mr. Thomas Girtin for
their invaluable assistance in the production
of this book.

Contents

6   Foreword

8   Clothworkers' Hall – a Building Tradition

27   Behind the Scenes

45   The Entrance Hall

61   The Court Suite

91   The Ceremonial Rooms

142   Acknowledgements

Foreword

It was with great pleasure that I accepted an invitation to write a short foreword to this book, as the Chairmanship of The Hall Refurbishment Committee has been one of the most exciting and satisfying tasks that I have ever undertaken.

When the Committee was set up it was known that the oil-fired boilers in the basement of Clothworkers' Hall were due for replacement and also that a good deal of general redecoration was necessary. Widely varying opinions were held by members of the Court as to what else further than this ought to be done. For example, air conditioning in the Ceremonial Rooms was considered to be essential by some and an extravagance by others; showers in the changing rooms were wanted by some and considered unnecessary by others; a serious study was made (and rejected) of building on a new top storey of bedrooms; and, of course, there were conflicting ideas for lighting, furnishings, and colour schemes.

It is remarkable that, after a life of nearly five years, the Committee completed the two phases of its work in a spirit of tolerance and without acrimony. It was very fortunate in its choice of advisers with whom relations were a model of harmony. It was also fortunate that the bulk of the many projects which were considered could be fitted into the programme, as the Company's financial position was sound enough to contemplate the very considerable cost involved. There were inevitably those who felt that the scale of expenditure was unjustified. I took a different view.

These days people are apt to belittle the ability of British craftsmen and consider that 'Art stopped short in the cultivated court of the Empress Josephine'. The vast majority of the furniture and fittings were made in Britain to the very high standards required by our architects; and those who examine their work cannot help but feel that today's craftsmen are every bit as talented as their predecessors. In my opinion the refurbishment has been well worth while, if only to give employment to these masters of their various trades as, sadly, there are few today that can afford to patronise the arts and crafts as in days gone by. Earlier this year we were pleased to entertain some of these craftsmen at Clothworkers' Hall and to let them see how their handiwork has helped to embellish the building. I know that this occasion was very much appreciated.

Nicholas Thompson of Donald W. Insall and Associates Ltd., who was in charge of the whole refurbishment project, has often been present at the Hall to explain his ideas and to give the Committee and the Court of The Clothworkers' Company expositions of his proposals, illustrated by slides. Everybody has always found these presentations absolutely fascinating. In particular his talk on 19 March this year, prior to the Refurbishment celebratory luncheon, was so enthralling that the Court agreed that the text should be printed and incorporated with appropriate photographs in a permanent record of the Hall Refurbishment. This volume is the result of that resolution and a copy of it is being sent to every Clothworker. In adapting his talk for publication, Mr Thompson has extended the scope of his subject by including a chapter on the Company's earlier Halls to set the recent Refurbishment of our sixth Hall in its historical context.

In the year that I was Master of our Company, 1983–84, I was privileged to be entertained in many of the other City Livery Company Halls and I must admit to feeling then that Clothworkers' Hall was not quite up to the standard of some of the others. I certainly do not feel this way today. Since the Refurbishment was completed in 1986 we have a Hall which perpetuates much of the Clothworker tradition and of which every member of the Company can feel proud. This was proved on a broader stage when, in 1987, the project received the City Heritage Award.

I only hope that, in the future, it will be possible for more members of the public to visit our Clothworker family home and share with us the enjoyment of its new-found beauty.

James Westoll
Chairman of The Hall Refurbishment Committee

1 November 1987.

I   Clothworkers' Hall
a Building Tradition

When on 17 July 1956 Her Royal Highness Princess Marina, Duchess of Kent, laid the foundation stone of the present Clothworkers' Hall, she referred in her speech to 'the remarkable continuity of institutions of which we in this country are so rightly proud'. On that summer day the Hall site off Mincing Lane had been in the possession of The Clothworkers' Company, and the Shearmen before them, for five hundred years and this was the Company's sixth Hall to be built upon it. As Thomas Girtin has shown in his comprehensive history of the Company, *The Golden Ram*, from which much of the material in this chapter is drawn, the Clothworkers have always been typical of their times. Through a combination of pragmatism and respect for tradition, they have ensured the continuity of the Company, evolving from a protective trade guild in medieval times to the valued and responsible charitable organisation which is their principal role today. Throughout the Company's history and work, its Halls have been central to its activities, for business and for pleasure. And in their design and furnishings, these buildings have been symbolic of the Company's purpose and traditions, expressive of its remarkable continuity.

Originally members of the Livery Companies met in their own houses or in local religious houses, but increased funds and the need for more commodious surroundings led them to seek permanent premises to serve as their Halls. The Clothworkers have been fortunate in always having their own. When they received their charter of incorporation in 1528 as 'the Guild or Fraternity of the Assumption of the Blessed Virgin Mary of Clothworkers in the City of London', they were in fact an amalgamation of two older Companies, the Fullers and the Shearmen, both of whom had Halls of their own. Just as the new Company succeeded to the precedence of the Shearmen in the City, becoming the last of the twelve so-called Great Companies, so it also adopted the Shearmen's Hall in Mincing Lane as its home. The deed dated 15 July 1456, which conveyed the site to a private group of Shearmen (for that Company had no charter), is still in the Clothworkers' possession.

Nothing is known of the first Hall, except that it was used for social occasions. Dinners were held there and pageants performed at Midsummer, when twenty-four men in straw hats held the cressets that flared outside it all the midsummer night long. The Clothworkers, perhaps finding the Hall too small for their needs, first added a Parlour in 1538. Ten years later, in 1548, they decided to rebuild completely, selling a parcel of land they owned in the City to pay for it. Something of the appearance of this new Hall can be gleaned from the surviving accounts of the tradesmen who built it and from descriptions of improvements carried out in the 1590s. It would appear to have been constructed as a timber-frame infilled with brick, and was ready for occupation by 1549. Again it comprised principally a Hall and a Parlour, the respective antecedents of the Ceremonial Rooms and the Court Suite of today's building, for while the Hall was devoted to the public and social meetings of the Company, the Parlour was where the Court of the Company met to carry out its business. The Hall itself would have been of the collegiate type, entered through a screen at one end and quite possibly with an open timber roof.

Clearly this building was somewhat short of domestic offices and perhaps rather basically finished, for in 1594 it was reported that there could be no dinner, 'only a drinking for that the hall and parlour and all the house is in such order that there cannot be any dressing of meat there or provision for that purpose'. So the parlour was to be panelled with wainscot and 'to be ceiled plain white with roses according to the former proportion'. In the last year of the century, the Hall itself was redecorated, 'the upper part in perspective work', its screens painted and gilded, and provision made of forty buckets decorated with the arms of The Clothworkers' Company. At the same time paving was laid in the garden and the flower beds stocked anew with herbs and flowers. But although now much enhanced, the Hall was perhaps still not as large as was desirable and the Clothworkers became particularly concerned about this after they had admitted the King (James I) to the Freedom of the Company in 1607. The increased status which they must have derived from this was perhaps what led to their decision to extend the building 'in length one bay at the upper end, more windows for light made on the sides, a louver to be made on the top thereof and a gallery all along on the north side of the garden with a return eastwards to beautify the said Hall and garden and specially the prospect of the parlour which now by the ruinousness of the houses directly opposite northwards and north of the prospect of the parlour is very unseemly besides the discommodity of overlooking the said garden from the said houses'.

This would seem to have been the limit to the building's capacity for enlargement, so that, when further consideration for change was given in 1633 and the Company's surveyor reported that 'the walls of the said Hall are much defective and cracked, the windows unfashionable and the whole frame uncomely and without ornament', the decision was taken to rebuild completely and on a larger scale. This was speedily done and the new Hall was complete within the year, even to the weather vane upon the lantern roof. As a pattern for the wainscotting, a room at the Antwerp Tavern was copied. At the upper end of the Hall were erected two statues by the carver Nicholas Stone, at a cost of fifty pounds. Almost certainly these would have been of James I and Charles I, for statues of both these kings were features of the Halls which followed. This, the third Hall on the site, survived the ensuing Civil War, when the Company joined the rest of the City in support of Parliament, who requisitioned the building as an Office of Sequestration.

By the Restoration, the Clothworkers were firmly in support of the monarch, and the Hall was the scene of great feasting, first in 1660 to honour General Monk and then two years later when the Company entertained the King and Queen, the Queen Mother and the Duke of York. But such jollity was soon to be cut short by the Plague. The Clothworkers ceased to hold meetings at the Hall and gave up their entertainments, voting that one third of what they would have spent on feasting should go to the relief of the afflicted. The last of the great dinners in their new Hall may therefore already have been held, for the Plague was followed closely by the Great Fire of 1666, which 'raged for five days and destroyed the whole City proper between the Tower and the Temple'. Thirteen thousand houses and ninety churches were lost and so was Clothworkers' Hall. Samuel Pepys, who was to be elected the Company's Master in 1677, saw the Hall burning like the wick of a lamp 'on fire these three days and nights in one body of Flame—it being the cellar, full of Oyle'.

Not only was the Hall lost, but many other of the Company's properties as well, and the Court decreed that, in view of the loss of rent from which their charitable grants were usually made, there should be 'no money or annuity to be paid to any person whatsoever by the Company without further order of this Court'. The site was cleared and, while plans were made for the rebuilding of the Hall, the Company met at the houses of its members. An early start on the new Hall was made possible by the generous offer of Sir Dennis Gawden to undertake immediately the building of the Parlour and Kitchen from his own pocket and to recover the cost from the Company at a later date. By 1668, the year following Gawden's election as Master, the Parlour was in use and probably the Hall too. This building survived longer than any other Hall to date and the appearance of its Livery Hall can be largely appreciated from two watercolours showing it in 1856 and 1857, when it was about to be demolished. It was described by Hatton in his *New View of London* in 1708 as 'a noble rich building. The Hall is . . . a lofty Room, adorned with wainscot to the ceiling, where is curious Fret-work. The Screen at the South End is of Oak, adorned with four Pilasters, their Entablature and Compass Pediment is of the Corinthian Order enriched with their Arms and Palm Branches. The west end is adorned with the Figures of King James I and King Charles I, richly carved as big as the Life in their Robes, with Regalia, all gilt with Gold, where is a Spacious Window of Stained Glass. . . .'

Very little change seems to have been made to the fourth Hall during its first hundred years, but in 1768 and 1773 considerable rebuilding and redecorating took place. Clearly it must have been around this time that the ceiling which appears in the nineteenth century watercolours was installed. At the same time new furniture was supplied by Liveryman Francis Pyner and, while the alterations were taking place, the Company dined at the London Tavern.

Something of the arrangement and use of the building can be gained from a contemporary description of a grand entertainment given to the Dukes of Kent and Sussex in 1814, following the First Treaty of Paris. The Master and the Wardens 'with a Military Band of Music were in the Lobby in the Hall to greet their Royal Highnesses who arrived a little after 3 o'clock and were conducted first into the Long Parlour and then up Stairs into the Court Room where they conversed with great Affability with the Lord Mayor'. At half past four dinner was announced and they proceeded into the Great Hall, the Upper and Under Beadle leading the way their their staves, 'the Royal Dukes supporting the Lord Mayor on their Arms, right and left. The tables were ornamented with Arches and Frames of Pastework and decorated with artificial Fruits and Flowers. The Dinner consisted of everything in Season; and the wines were such only (Madeira and Port) as the Company use at their Entertainments at this Hall'. There were many speeches, all subsequently printed, and a number of toasts, including one to 'The Emperor of Russia and our brave allies (Nine cheers) . . . In the course of this Entertainment several appropriate songs and glees were sung by the professional singers and the whole concluded with the greatest Harmony and Satisfaction.'

In 1824 Samuel Angell was appointed Surveyor to the Company. Angell had been a pupil of Thomas Hardwick, whose son, Philip, also a pupil of his father's, was later to design Goldsmiths' Hall. Angell's appointment to the Company was a long one and the first thirty years of it were spent in maintaining the seventeenth century Hall. Clearly the building was becoming progressively unsound. The Company was, however, going through a period of some financial embarrassment, and it was not until 1840 when the strenuous endeavours of Thomas Massa Alsager, who had served as Master in 1836–37, had brought about a sufficient measure of recovery, that some £1,200 could be spent on repairs. More drastic changes had to wait until the prosperous years of the 1850s.

In 1855 Samuel Angell was asked to make a full report on the condition of the building, whose foundations he was to find had 'mouldered and trembled'. The poor state of the Hall was in part attributed to the haste in which it had been built following the Great Fire and to the 'difficulty in obtaining a sufficiency of good materials upon so sudden and large a demand'. In addition to the deterioration of soft and ill-burned bricks, 'the timbers of chestnut had the dry-rot and were in a fearful state of security'. The old Hall was condemned with some reluctance and plans drawn up for an impressive replacement, the fifth Hall to be built on the site. A contract for its erection was let to John Jay for £33,846 in September 1856, and the Company moved out to Barbers' Hall, which it rented until its return in April 1859. The new Hall was officially opened on 27 March 1860 in the presence of the Prince Consort on whom the Freedom and Honorary Livery of the Company were bestowed. The occasion was reported in *The Times* the following day, and a full description of the building published:

> The New Hall . . . is one of the finest of which the City can boast. Boldly carved enrichments adorn the facade which is of the Italian style of Architecture of the Renaissance Period. The Arms of the Company surmount a lofty portal with bronze gates in the centre. This leads to an arched corridor and vestibule which form the approach to the entrance Hall over the doorways of which are four relievi executed in Caen stone by Mr. C. Kelsey, representing the attributes of the Company—Loyalty, Integrity, Industry and Charity. From the entrance hall—from which it is partially separated by coupled columns—springs the grand staircase. On each side

THE CRAFTSMAN IN THE CITY

The Livery Hall of the fourth Clothworkers' Hall was built *c.* 1668, but shown here in a watercolour of 1856 by P. W. Justyne. The ceiling was put in during the late 18th century. Most of the pieces of plate depicted remain in the Company's possession.

CLOTHWORKERS' HALL

A dinner in the fourth Hall. On either side of the display of plate can be seen the statues of James I and Charles I. The stained glass of the windows shown in this view is not an accurate representation of what was there.

of it, on the ground floor, are the several offices of the Company for the purpose of business. This floor contains, also, the culinary departments—essential portion of a City Hall—on the construction and arrangement of which no ordinary amount of care and skill has evidently been bestowed.

At the foot of the grand staircase are two bronze griffins, admirable both for execution and design, the work of Mr. Kelsey.

On the first landing are to be seen the Royal Arms in alto relievo and in all the propriety of heraldic emblazonment. A lofty pendentive dome surmounts the staircase itself which leads to the piano nobile where, as in Italian palaces, are the State apartments. Here are to be found the reception rooms of the Livery, and a drawing room for the Court of Assistants and their guests. Here also stands the banqueting hall, the chief feature of the building. It is a room of noble proportions and perfect harmony of design. In extreme length it is 80 feet, 40 feet wide and 40 feet in height. Corinthian engaged columns of Aberdeen granite, highly polished and resting on granite pedestals, with a stylobate of richly veined Devonshire marble, divide it into five bays at the sides and three at the ends.

Above the entablature surmounting these columns is an attic from which springs a coved ceiling. Of this ceiling the cove is pierced with semi-circular windows in which are represented the arms of the Twelve City Companies beautifully executed by Mr. Lavers.

Female figures, in alto relievo, emblematical of twelve of the principal commercial Cities of the Empire adorn the spaces between these windows . . .

There were, *The Times* noted, five other stained glass windows with the arms of prominent members of the Company as well as two statues, of James I and Charles I. Although as yet the gilding and enrichments in colour were incomplete it was reported that 'the general effect of this portion of the building is somewhat like that produced by the gallery of the Hotel de Ville in Paris'. The decorations were finally completed at a further cost nearing £5,000 in 1870.

Despite an idea, floated in 1924 but not carried out, for rebuilding Clothworkers' Hall on the third and fourth floors of a new building which was to contain commercial offices at the lower levels, the Victorian Hall continued to serve the Company until

CLOTHWORKERS' HALL

Above: ground floor plan of the fourth Clothworkers' Hall.

Below: ground floor plan of the fifth Clothworkers' Hall. The Drawing Room and the Livery Hall (running north south) were on the floor above.

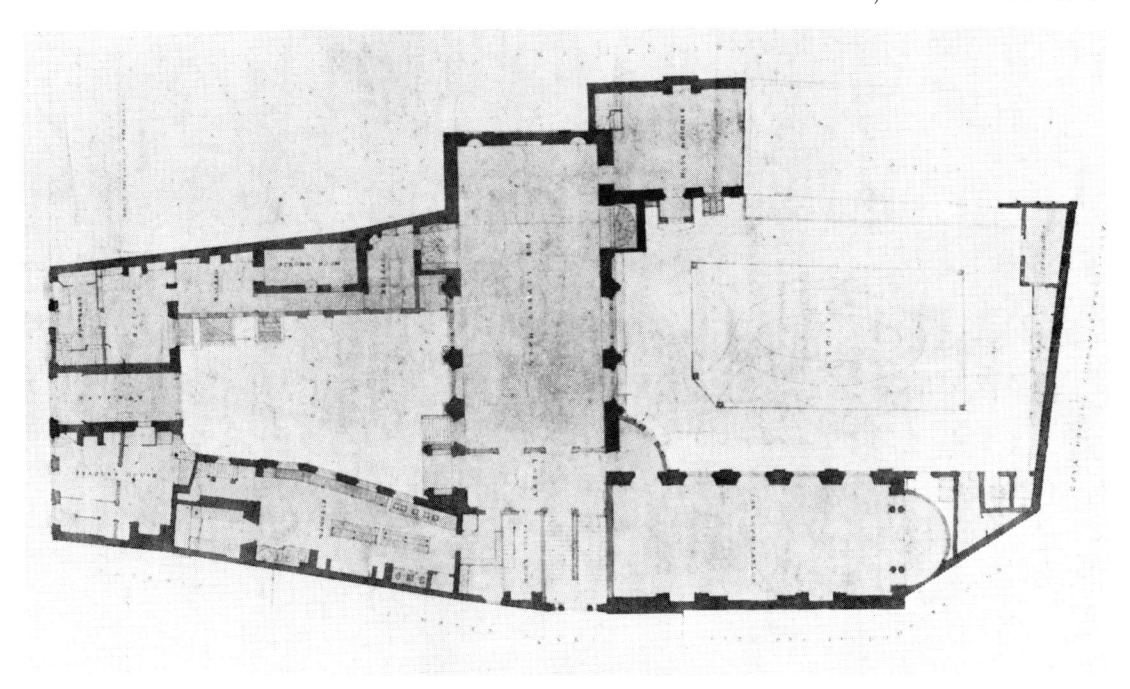

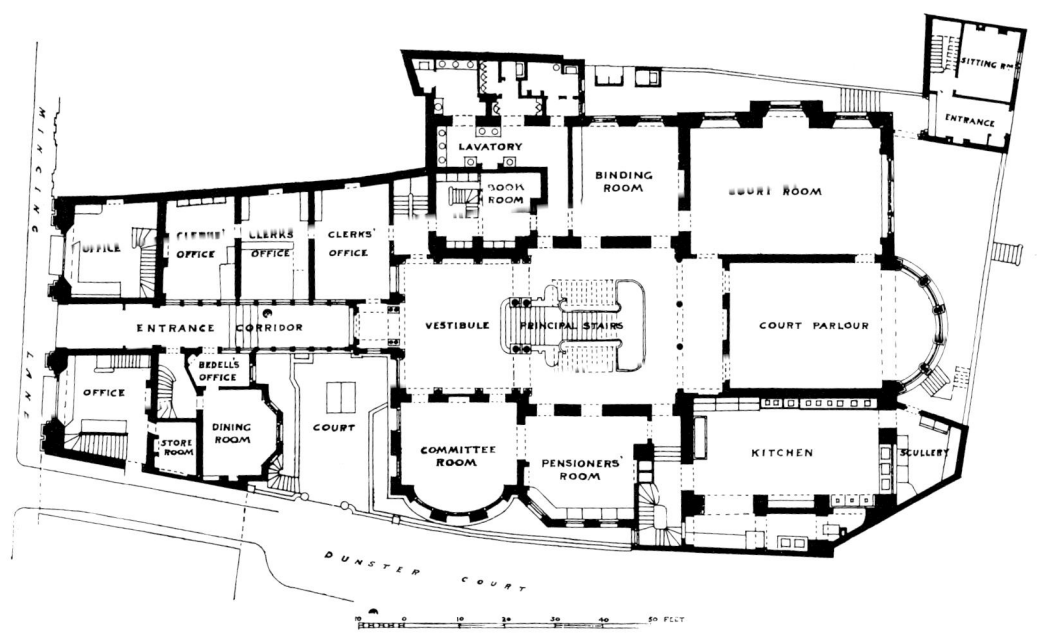

THE CRAFTSMAN IN THE CITY

The Drawing Room of the Victorian Hall, c. 1916. The ceiling has been copied in the Reception Room of the present Hall. The mural at the end of the room depicted the story of Edward Osborne.

Above: design drawing showing the east side of the Victorian Livery Hall.

Below: the Victorian Livery Hall, a view published by *The Builder* in 1916.

Hitler's air raids meant that the buildings of the City were once more under threat. In 1939 measures were taken against the risks in prospect. It was agreed to leave Company plate, recently sent to the United States for an exhibition, in America. An alternative strong-room was provided at Hay's Wharf for the famous Pepys Cup and some of the best plate that remained in England. Duplicates of the Company's records were made

CLOTHWORKERS' HALL

The Grand Staircase of the Victorian Hall. The panel above the door to the left of the staircase was one of four, another of which has been incorporated in the Court Corridor of the present Hall, above the door to the Court Luncheon Room.

on microfilm and stored at Morden. The Hall was offered as a billet for 150 or even 200 soldiers in an emergency.

On a number of occasions during 1940 and in the early part of 1941 the Hall narrowly escaped destruction by enemy action. But during the night of Saturday 10 May 1941, another spectacular raid lasting five hours devastated the City. No fire-watching force could hope to stem the destruction, unknown on such a scale since the Great Fire had destroyed the third Hall. By 2 o'clock on Sunday morning the Hall was ringed by fire, but still stood intact among the flames. By 7 o'clock it was clear that the Hall was doomed; and it took until 5 o'clock that afternoon for the flames to be finally extinguished. Only the strongrooms and safes had resisted the fire. The plate, both at the Hall and at Hay's Wharf, had escaped; and together with the Charters, some hundred boxes of title deeds and account and minute books dating from 1528 had survived. So also had the main doors, the coat of arms over the entrance, and the four wall plaques depicting Industry, Integrity, Charity and Loyalty.

The loss of the Hall was but one setback which the Company was to suffer as a result of the War. From a corporate income which in 1942 had fallen to about two-thirds, and in 1943 to less than half, the figure at which it had stood before the War, the Clothworkers contrived to play the part they had always played, although it sometimes proved necessary to modify their benefactions. Gradually normality began to return, though in one sense nothing could really be normal again until the Company had a Hall once more.

In formulating ideas for the new building, the Company decided to revive the concept put forward in 1924 that part of the site should be used for commercial offices. Plans were prepared by the architect Henry Tanner; and after his death Whinney Son and Austen Hall were appointed, H. Austen Hall taking charge. This practice had been formed originally to act for the Midland Bank and had collaborated with Sir Edwin Lutyens on three of the four Bank projects he designed. In addition to Clothworkers' Hall, it was responsible after the War for the design of a new Hall for The Carpenters' Company and carried out the refurbishment of Fishmongers' Hall. Progress from first ideas to the opening of the new Clothworkers' building took some thirteen years, a protracted business, drawn out by a number of factors, not least of all the difficulty in determining the right scheme for the site. Tanner, before his death, had provided some five schemes and Austen Hall was to continue the process of refinement. The Company decided it could only spend on its new Hall what it would ultimately receive by way of compensation from the War Damage Commission; and this amount could not be agreed until a building licence was awarded. In the meantime increases in the cost of building dictated further changes of plan. Moreover there were negotiations to be carried out for widening Dunster Court and for constructing an exit road into Mark Lane. By 1950 planning permission was granted and the Company applied for

An unexecuted proposal for the first floor of the post-war Hall. Many of the architectural features of the present Reception Room and Library relate to this plan and make more sense in the arrangement as shown here. Note also the Supper Room at the east end of the Livery Hall, where now there is a flat for the Beadle.

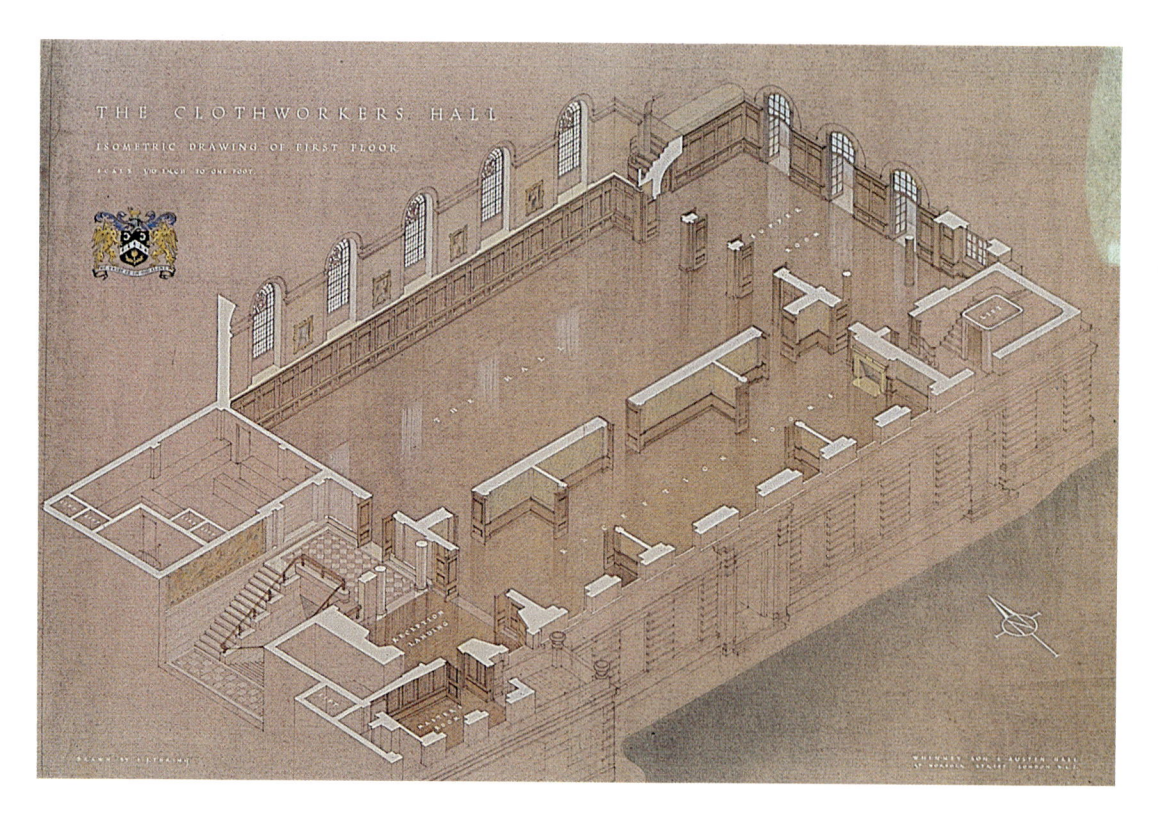

a building licence, which ultimately was granted just a few months before the war-time regulation calling for it was lifted. By March 1955 tenders were received for the new building, and that submitted by Humphreys Ltd was accepted. Between then and July 1956, when the Duchess of Kent was invited to lay the foundation stone, the Company's Hall Rebuilding Committee met regularly to determine how to keep within the budget in the face of rising costs. Ultimately it was many of the finishes and embellishments which formed part of the architect's original concept that had to be sacrificed.

On 16 June 1955 the Clerk wrote to Austen Hall suggesting that savings could be made by replacing the marble floor in the Entrance Hall with wood, by omitting the fireplaces and flues planned for the reception rooms and elsewhere, by having the floor

CLOTHWORKERS' HALL

The Livery Hall of the sixth Clothworkers' Hall in 1967.

of the balcony over the Livery Hall built at one level rather than in tiers, and by omitting acoustic ceilings, panelling in the Master's Room and rustication and carving on the east elevation. When a sub-committee met in early July they agreed that, in addition to these items, a further saving of £68,570 could be made 'without detriment to the scheme as a whole' by cutting out certain special finishings, screens and doors intended for the reception rooms, carving and sculpture, a chair lift, stained glass windows in the Livery Hall and gilding on the gates. In March 1956, by which time building work

The Reception Room of the present Hall in 1967.

had started and delays in steel deliveries were being experienced, estimates were again revised to affect further savings by omitting damask wall linings in the Reception Room and Committee Room, and panelling on the Reception Landing, in the Court Room and in the Court Corridor. There were no longer to be bronze lamp standards on the principal staircase and gold leaf enrichment was omitted throughout.

In its somewhat depleted form, the new Clothworkers' Hall eventually emerged, lightly clad in 'Georgian' dress, expressing at least on the surface historical continuity rather than dramatic change or innovation. Its links with the destroyed Hall were stressed

Exterior of the Hall in 1967.

by the re-use of salvaged elements such as the entrance doors and the stone coat-of-arms above them, and by quoting precedents in such new-built features as the Reception Room ceiling, which was copied from the Victorian Drawing Room. Though simpler than Austen Hall had originally intended, the Livery Hall itself clearly echoed its predecessors, with its five great windows and, as in the seventeenth century, panelling on the walls. Although the new building was now entered from Dunster Court, where before the entrance had been in Mincing Lane, Austen Hall had also maintained the same important east to west axis linking the principal rooms on two floors as before. Once again the Hall was also to be a symbol of the Company in its decorative use of the coat of arms, and of motifs derived from the habick and the teasel, tools used by the clothworker in his craft. Below the surface the building was very much of its own time. Constructed with a steel frame and concrete floors, it had underfloor heating and mechanical ventilation carried through the walls in a maze of metal ducts. Beyond the areas used for Court business and public and ceremonial occasions on the ground and first floors, a suite of modern offices was provided for the Company's use on the second and third floors, with a further floor above that for commercial letting, accessible from an independent entrance in Mincing Lane. Plant rooms, kitchens and domestic offices for the Company were located in the basement.

In resolving how best to use the funds available, it had clearly been essential to get the basic scheme right and to build it well. This the Company was able to do: the Hall continues to be effective in use and its construction has stood the test of time. But whereas the Company could use the building without some of the finer finishes, furniture had to be provided from the start. For many of the essential items, the Clothworkers went to the firm of Gordon Russell. The pieces supplied were very much of their time, more reflective perhaps of contemporary ideas about design than of the classical setting of Austen Hall's building. A few special pieces, however, were designed by the architect for the Livery Hall and these were more in keeping.

The building was officially opened in April 1958 by the Princess Royal (Princess Mary), who was thereupon admitted as an Honorary Freewoman of the Company. Following this, improvements and embellishments to the Hall continued. In some cases these were to make good the omissions of the original building or losses from the old Hall. The splendid series of five stained glass windows designed by Hugh Easton for the Livery Hall was a case in point; and when in 1966 some of the principal rooms were re-decorated, gilding was added to the ceilings and cornices. Throughout these years the Company's stock of furniture and paintings was being augmented by special commissions, new purchases and bequests and gifts from members. The Clothworkers were settling into their sixth Hall and making it their home.

II   Behind the Scenes

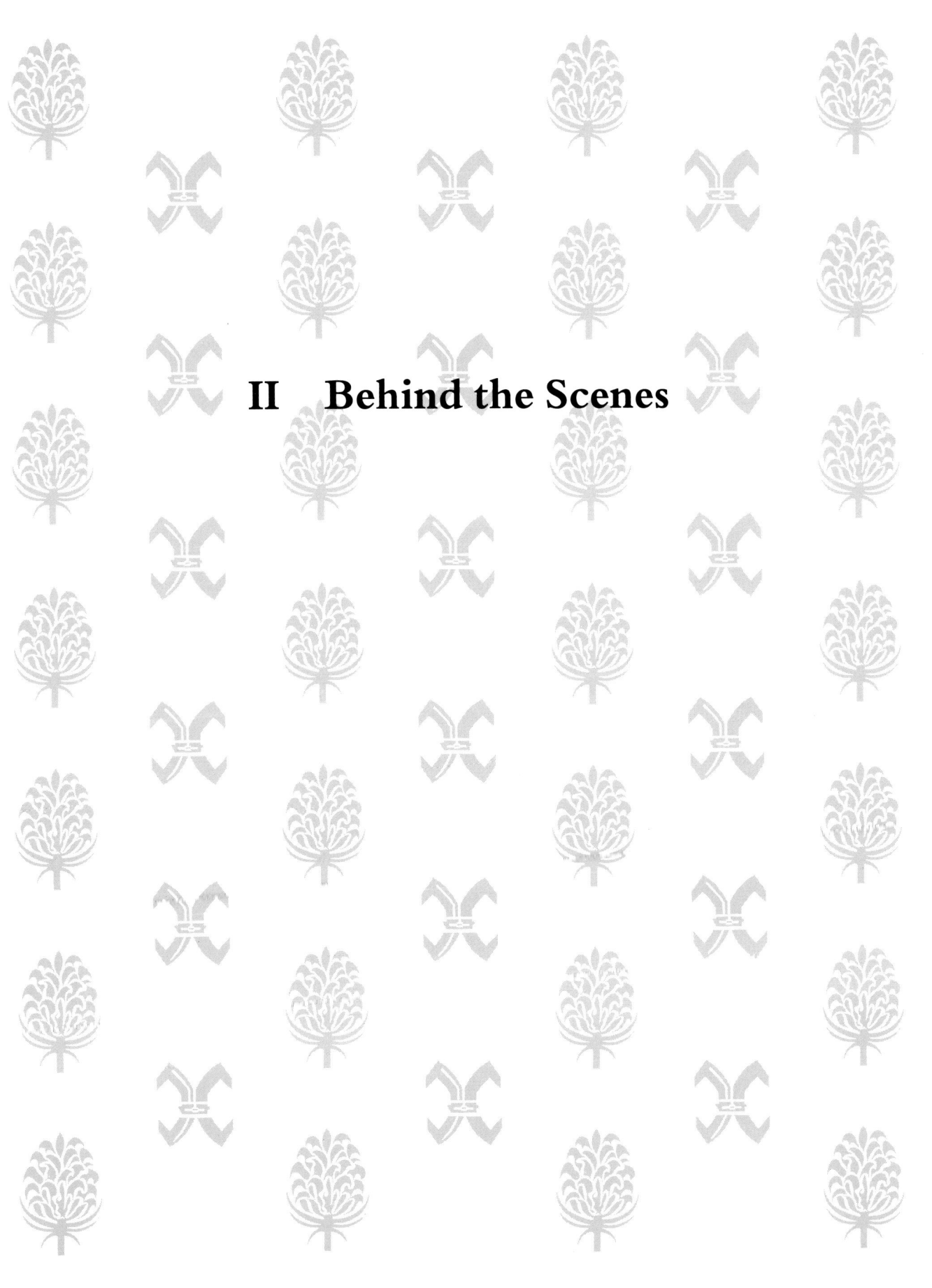

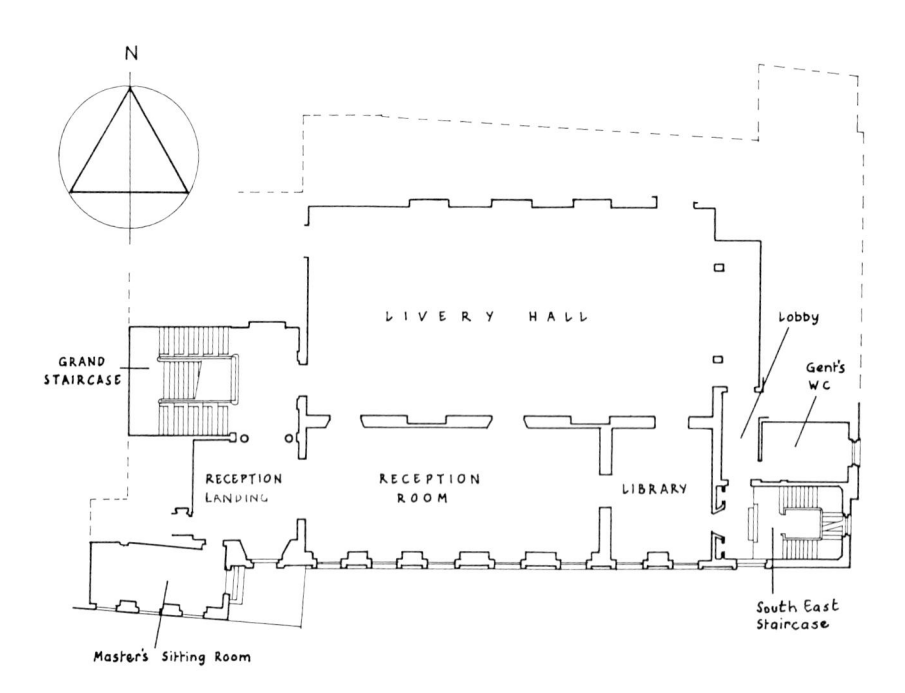

N

GRAND STAIRCASE

LIVERY HALL

Lobby

Gent's WC

RECEPTION LANDING

RECEPTION ROOM

LIBRARY

South East Staircase

Master's Sitting Room

FIRST FLOOR

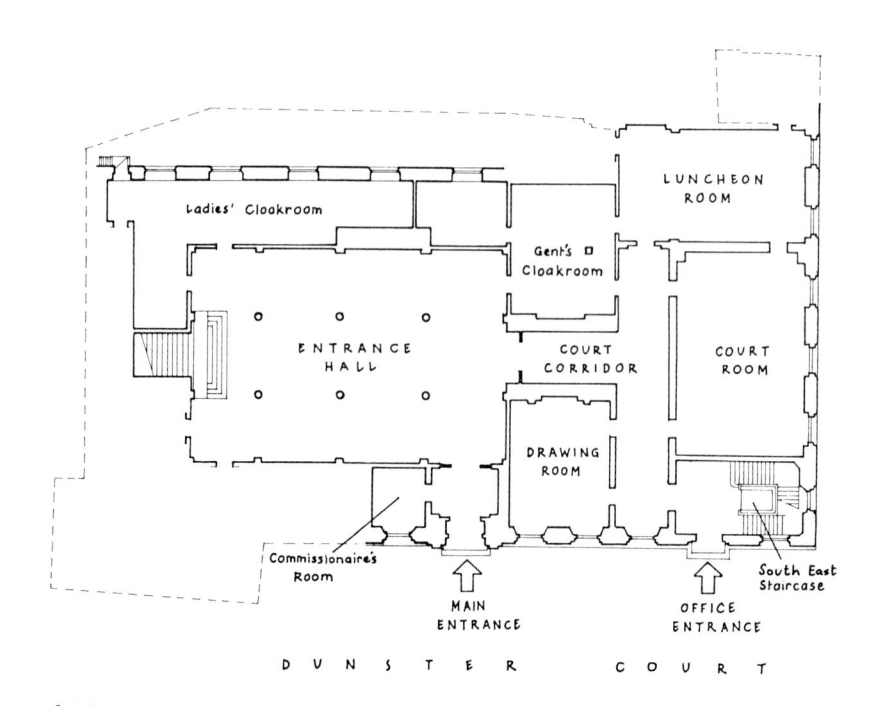

Ladies' Cloakroom

LUNCHEON ROOM

Gent's Cloakroom

ENTRANCE HALL

COURT CORRIDOR

COURT ROOM

DRAWING ROOM

Commissionaire's Room

MAIN ENTRANCE

OFFICE ENTRANCE

South East Staircase

DUNSTER COURT

GROUND FLOOR

CLOTHWORKERS' HALL

Ground and first floor plans of the
present Hall before refurbishment.

By the early 1980s it was becoming apparent to officers and members of The Clothworkers' Company that their Hall, by then twenty-five years old, was in need of some attention. Several elements of the original building, such as boilers and other services, were due for replacement; and there was a feeling that a measure of air-conditioning should be introduced to maintain comfortable conditions during functions held in high summer. There was scope too for further improvements to bring the Hall into line with modern standards and for redecorating its principal rooms, where paintwork, carpets and curtains had become worn or faded. With the completion in prospect of a major development project in the City, the Company felt that it could now afford to embark on a programme of refurbishment.

During 1983 a team of appropriate consultants was selected by the Company and appointed for the project under the co-ordination of Richard Ellis as project managers. Donald W. Insall and Associates Ltd. were to be the architects, Sir Frederick Snow and Partners the consulting services engineers, Andrews, Kent and Stone the consulting structural engineers, and Gardiner and Theobald the quantity surveyors. The first task was to determine exactly what should be done, and the next few months were devoted to a programme of survey, analysis and briefing, followed by the drafting of costed proposals for consideration by a Hall Refurbishment Committee and ultimately by the Court of the Company.

From a building services point of view it was agreed that the old oil-fired boilers should be replaced with new ones fuelled by gas, and that additional environmental control should be provided by means of individual fan-coil units in the Livery Hall and Reception Room, where the largest concentrations of people could be expected. The electrical distribution system had recently been renewed, so that changes here were generally limited to improvements in lighting and the replacement of switch plates and sockets to conform with the interior design proposals being formulated. Other recommendations included the overhaul of lifts, the installation of new systems for fire alarm, smoke detection and emergency lighting, and the removal of asbestos from the building in all areas where it would be disturbed by the works in prospect.

From an architectural point of view, Donald W. Insall and Associates admired Austen Hall's concept for the building, its classical inspiration and its articulate plan. The omitted details, however, were regretted; they would have finished the interior, and given much

Unsightly ventilation grilles in the Court Luncheon Room before refurbishment.

Above: a mixture of antique and 1950s furniture on the Reception Landing. Note the carpet incorporating habicks and teasels.

Below left: 1950s light fittings in the Court Room.

Below right: an unlined window in the Reception Room. Fresh air was supplied to the room through the slot behind the cornice.

needed character to the different spaces. Generally where the design had gone ahead as planned, the result had been successful: the Grand Staircase, for example, which exactly follows the original drawings, achieves a highly original and successful transition between the somewhat elemental Entrance Hall and the more fully classical interiors of the *piano nobile*. By contrast the Reception Room, based on the Drawing Room of the 1859 Hall, was clearly incomplete; and here, as in many of the rooms, the lack of any architectural lining to the window reveals and the hanging of curtains in slots behind the cornice did little for the proportions or the dignity of the interior.

In the absence of much of the originally intended detail and finishes, the 1950s services technology tended to assume an undue prominence, with ventilation grilles scattered about the place in a seemingly arbitrary fashion. Obviously it had not been possible to make the necessary savings at the time of building 'without detriment to the scheme as a whole' as had been thought; and it was resolved to make good the omissions, not necessarily exactly as intended in the 1950s, but certainly in the spirit of the original and to complement such detail and architectural character as the Hall had already been given.

With regard to furnishing the interiors, it seemed that in many cases neither the Gordon Russell furniture of the 1950s nor the antique pieces bequeathed to the Company sat very happily in the particular brand of neo-Georgian which Austen Hall had devised. The two types of furniture when mixed together had an even more bizarre effect. Some rationalisation was therefore needed, and it was agreed to consider, in many areas, new

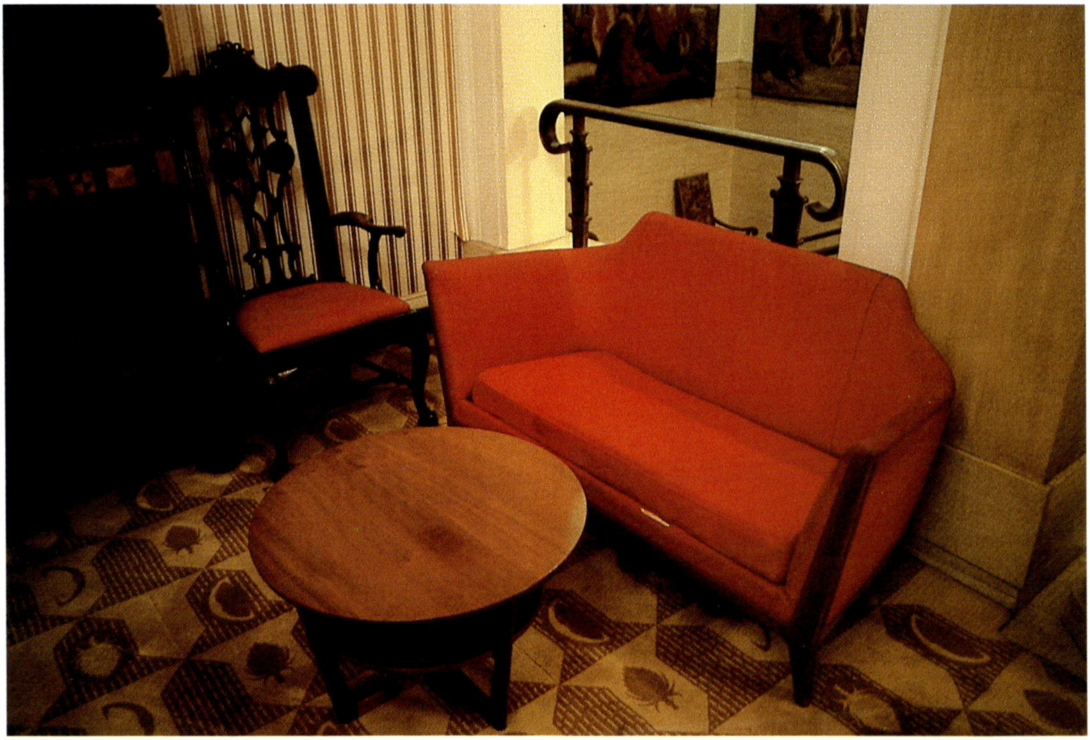

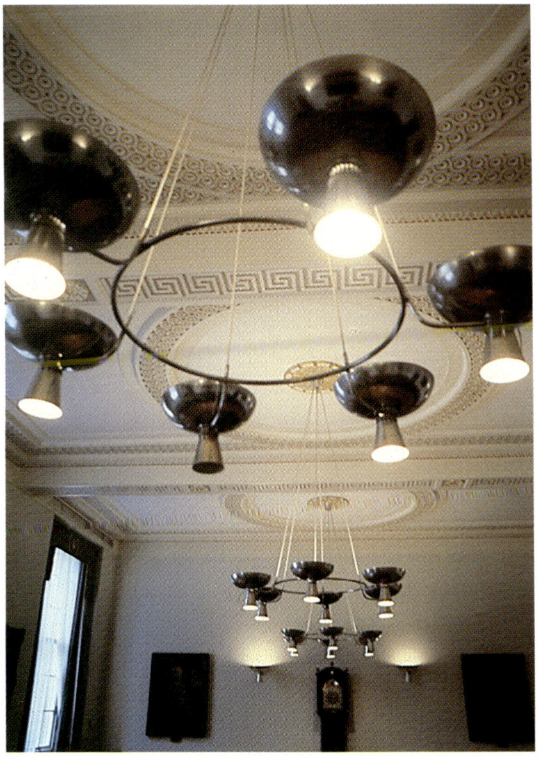

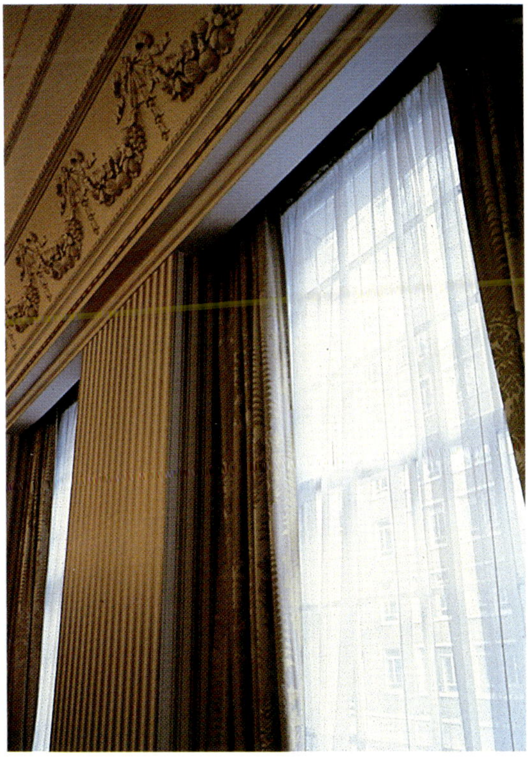

A hoist outside the Library window provided access to the Hall for materials from Dunster Court during the second refurbishment contract.

The churchyard was used as the contractors' compound during the refurbishment.

furniture, light fittings, carpets and fabrics that would conform with traditional designs. The two large suites of chairs and tables made for the Livery Hall and the Court Room, however, continued to serve their purpose well, and it was agreed that they should be retained.

Outside the principal areas, the interior design of the building was much plainer and more 'modern'; it was felt here that decorations and furnishings should reflect the change. It was further agreed that, where appropriate, the idea should be continued of incorporating in the decoration the motifs of The Clothworkers' Company—the habick, the teasel and the ram. These would help to express the symbolic nature of the Hall and make it personal to the Company.

The principal interiors to be tackled divided into three main groups arranged on two floors. On the ground floor was the Entrance Hall, with cloakrooms leading directly from it. In its simplicity this space provided an architectural foil to the other interiors and, by means of the important cross-axis through the building, linked the two other principal groups—the Court Suite on the ground floor and, via the Grand Staircase, the main Ceremonial Rooms on the first floor. Related to these areas, but outside them, were the South East Staircase which rose through the full six storeys of the building, the private flats used by the Master and the Clerk at the west end of the building, and the basement which contained extensive plant and service accommodation.

To permit the continuing use of the building, the work was planned in two phases, the first dealing principally with the basement, the main service plant and the Court Suite, and the second with the Entrance Hall, first floor Ceremonial Rooms, the flats and the South East Staircase. Higgs and Hill Management Contracting Ltd. won the two five-month contracts to carry out the construction work in 1985 and 1986 and, under their management, some eighteen sub-contracts were tendered for and let in each phase. At the end of each building period, time was allowed for furnishing the rooms, carried out as a series of direct contracts and appointments by the Company under the architects' direction. Before each phase of work, designs were agreed with the Hall Refurbishment Committee and then presented to the Court for its approval. Throughout the project, progress was monitored at monthly meetings under the chairmanship of the project manager and attended by officers of the Company, the appointed consultants and the management contractor. It was therefore a substantial team that emerged to

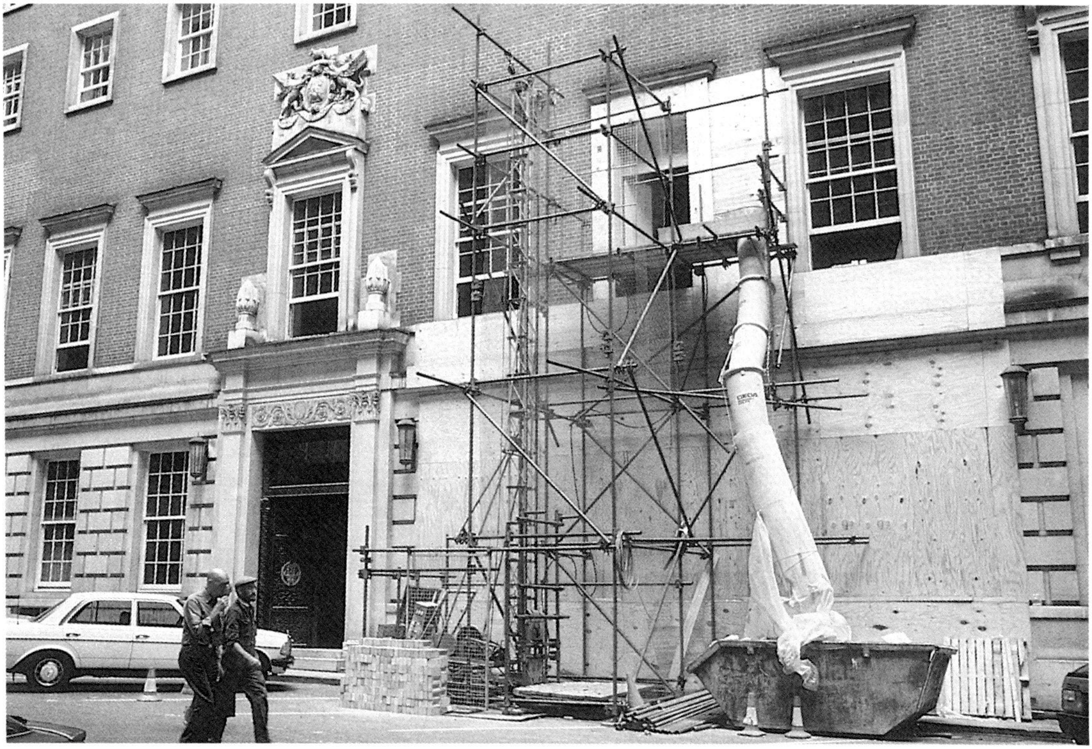

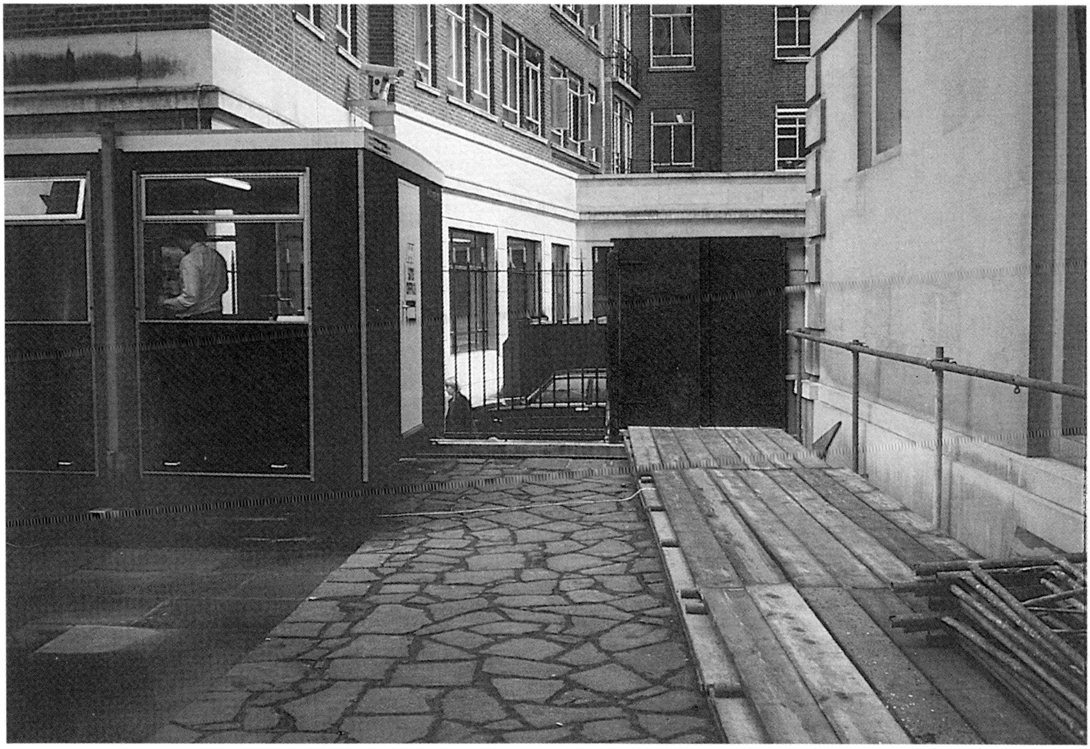

THE CRAFTSMAN IN THE CITY

Welding pipework in a basement plant room.

Mock-up of one of the new displays of Company plate being arranged in the strong room.

plan and execute the work in accordance with a very tight programme, devised to minimise disruption to the Company.

    The execution of the project was greatly helped by the existence of two vital pieces of private open space adjacent to the Hall. Dunster Court was the point from which access to the building was gained—during the first phase via the South East Staircase and the Court Corridor window for the ground floor, and via a trap in the pavement for services work in the basement. The Company continued to use the main entrance

BEHIND THE SCENES

Cutting curtains at Charles Hammond.

Wood-carving by Anthony Harrington.

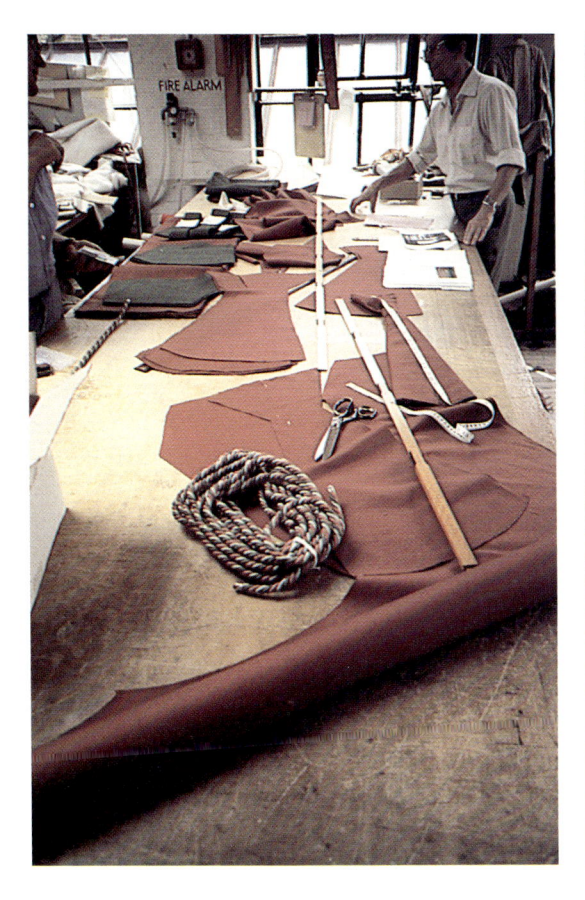

and the Ceremonial Rooms on the first floor. During the second phase, the main entrance was used for the contract, with materials conveyed to the first floor by means of a hoist outside the Library window. While this work was going on, the Company was able to make use of its newly refurbished Court Suite. During both periods the churchyard to the east of the building served as a compound for the offices and stores of Higgs and Hill and their sub-contractors.

The range of the work undertaken was extensive, demanding high levels of technical

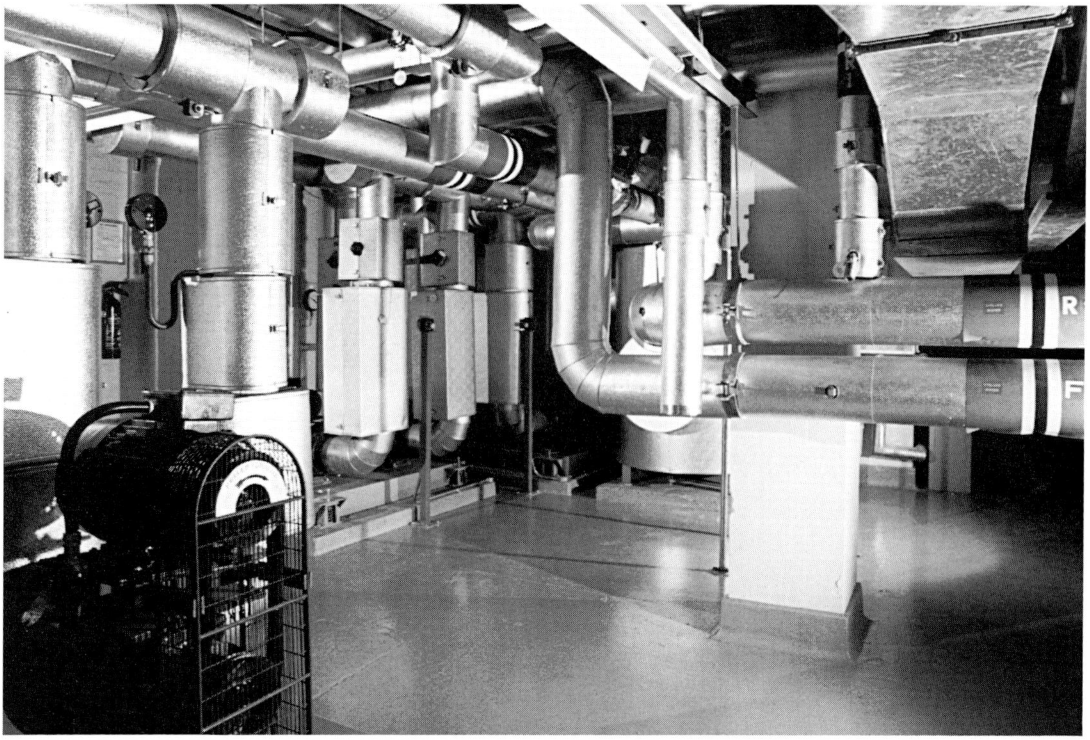

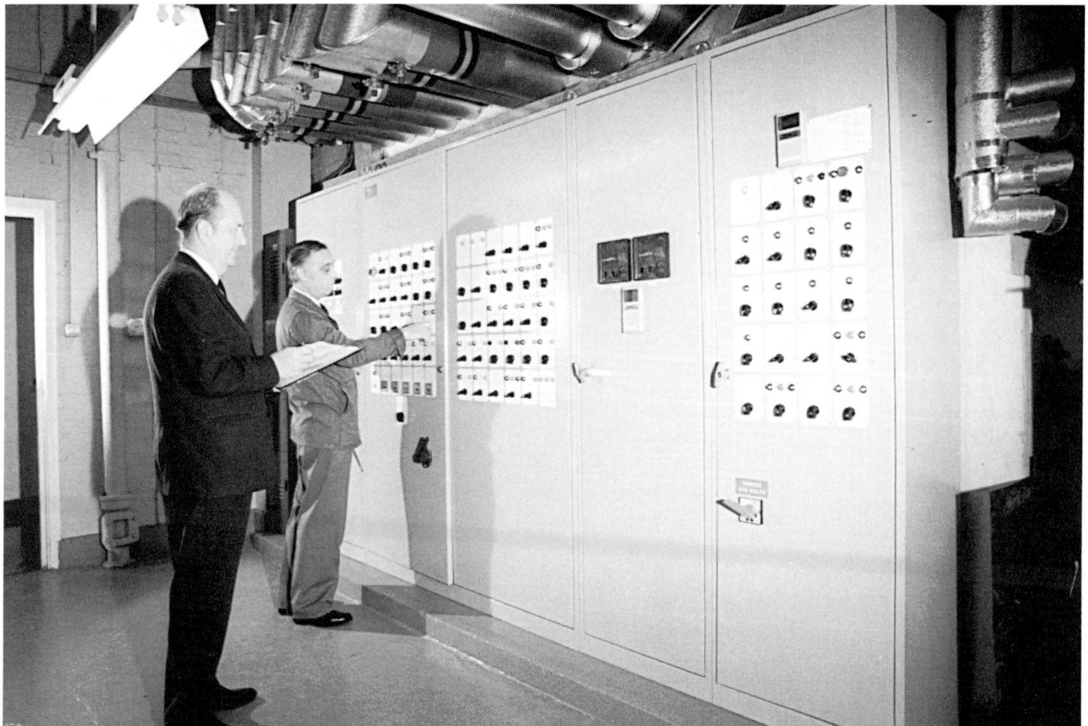

BEHIND THE SCENES

Inside the new ventilation plant room.

Checking the running of equipment at the main electrical control panel.

Regulating the gas-burners of the new boilers.

skill and craftsmanship. Moreover, since it was to take place in an existing and continuously occupied building, much sensitivity and tact, both architectural and personal, was needed. At one end of the work spectrum was the controlled removal of asbestos in pre-isolated areas, the feeding in of new ductwork and structural steel, the renewal of engineering services and wrestling with intractable plumbing. At the other end were more rarefied processes such as the weaving of silk damask and the making of curtains, fine wood-carving and the rearrangement of displays of the Company's plate.

The Ceremonial Rooms and the Court Suite are perhaps all that are seen by most visitors to Clothworkers' Hall; but much has been done outside these areas to make the accommodation more comfortable, more effective to use, and to bring it into line with modern standards. Fundamental to the whole project has been the considerable work done to the building services. Much of this is, of course, out of sight, with the main plant either in the basement where the new boiler house, electrical control room and ventilation plant are located, or on the roof where new chillers have been installed to serve the areas in which cooling facilities have been added. From these points pipes, ducts and conduits thread their way through the building to the various outlets where the energy generated is needed and harnessed. This was the work of Longstaff and Shaw Ltd. in the first phase and Matthew Hall Ltd. in the second, both aided by the invaluable knowledge of Patrick Walsh who had taken part in the building of the Hall during the 1950s and had thereafter been retained as the Company's resident engineer.

Behind the Livery Hall, T.A. Martin and Son Ltd., who carried out the general builder's work for both phases, replaced the unsatisfactory glazed roof of the main kitchen with a new solid and insulated one. In the basement, the hitherto disorientating East Corridor, which leads to the Staff Canteen and the Clerk's Dining Room, has been given a sense of place by removing a door half-way along its length and by adding new lighting. The space now provides an opportunity to display the Company's collection of pen and ink drawings of the City by Hanslip Fletcher. At the same time many of the basement service rooms were altered and re-equipped and the existing Livery changing rooms were re-cast and extended to include bath and shower rooms.

Most of the work in the basement took place during 1985. 1986 saw the redecoration of the South East Staircase and the refurbishment of the lift there. This included providing a new metal sheath for the shaft in place of the panels of wired glass, which had been impossible to clean from the inside. Mindful of the many different visitors to Clothworkers' Hall, and the Charities which it supports, the Company required that the new lift controls should be additionally identified in Braille and that some awkward steps on the first floor landing should be removed to allow easy wheel-chair access to the Ceremonial Rooms. Provision for wheel-chair users has also been made in the refurbishment of the lavatories on this stair. On the first floor and first floor mezzanine are the flats used by the Beadle and the Butler. Both are resident in the Hall and, for their greater comfort, air-conditioning has been provided. At the foot of the staircase, inside the east entrance to the building, is a new movable work-station for use by the Commissionaire. Fitted with its own lighting, heating and co-axial feed for closed circuit security

The new roof to the main kitchen on the north side of the Hall.

The east basement corridor before refurbishment.

Below: The corridor after removal of the door and the introduction of new lighting.

Above left: First floor lavatory before refurbishment.

Above right and below: Lavatories on the South-East Staircase after refurbishment.

South-East Staircase and lift after refurbishment.

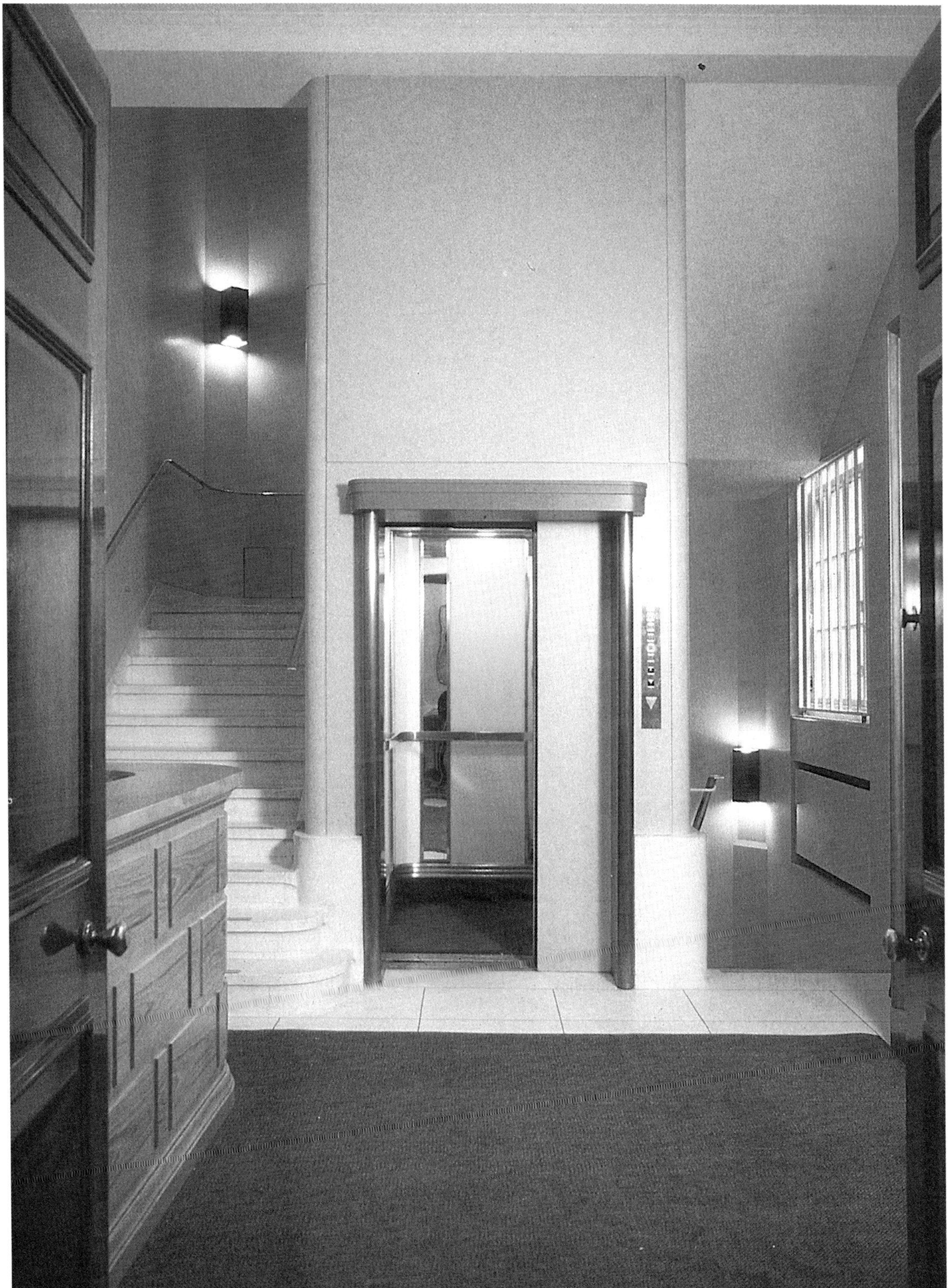

Ground Floor
THE
CLOTHWORKERS' COMPANY
RECEPTION SECOND FLOOR
PLEASE USE LIFT

BEHIND THE SCENES

New desk for the Commissionaire and doors to the Court Suite from the South-East Staircase.

The Master's sitting room. The panelled door at the back of the room is new.

monitors, it is part of a new suite of fittings made in teak for the more 'modern' interiors of the Hall.

At the west end of the building, the bedroom suites for the occasional use of the Master and the Clerk have been redecorated, and new furniture and furnishings supplied. Directly beneath the Master's bedroom is his sitting room, which has also been redecorated. Much of the former contents of the room have been reinstated, although the covers to seat furniture, the curtains and the carpet are new. In place of a plain painted door, a new panelled mahogany one now leads to a small kitchenette and washroom beyond.

Situated as it is directly off the first floor Reception Landing, the sitting room is something of a link between the private and public interiors of Clothworkers' Hall—the Ceremonial Rooms on the first floor, the Court Suite on the ground floor and the Entrance Hall which provides the prelude to them both.

III The Entrance Hall

THE CRAFTSMAN IN THE CITY

The Entrance Hall in 1983.

THE ENTRANCE HALL

Deliberately conceived as a foil for the richer interiors on the first floor and in the Court Suite to the east, the Entrance Hall had been nonetheless somewhat stark and bland, with little architectural detail to relieve the great expanses of blank wall. Although deriving, through the English eighteenth century and Palladio, from Roman precedents in its atrium form and its relationship to the rest of the building, there was little that was truly classical by way of detail. Its more 'modern' treatment seemed to derive from the 1930s and from buildings such as Grey Wornum's Royal Institute of British Architects of 1932–34. The use of marble, silver-bronze doors with etched-glass panels and even lighting in the form of huge glass 'poached-eggs' floating in the ceiling can all be seen at the RIBA. The combination of these features at Clothworkers' Hall in a series of more or less equal bays marked out by columns and pilasters extending both across and down the room, had resulted in a bewildering lack of direction. Furthermore the feel of the space was not helped by the very resonant acoustic, which made conversation difficult.

Attempts to humanise the space and give it interest had already been made by introducing some antique furniture and a display cabinet, and by lining the walls with panels of flock paper. The results had never been really satisfactory. As a large space for receiving visitors, the Entrance Hall was vital but, in the form in which it was in 1983, it was certainly under-exploited. A special acoustic study was carried out by Sound Research Laboratories Ltd., who advised that by treating the walls with acoustically-absorbent material and by partially carpeting the floor, the existing reverberation time could be halved. Such a recommendation dovetailed nicely with architectural proposals to rusticate the walls, to give interest and texture to the space without unduly softening it. Further articulation has now been provided by replacing the travertine cladding to the tops of the columns and pilasters with a darker marble, suggesting capitals, and by removing the circular lights from the centre two bays and providing cornice lighting to a slightly higher level of ceiling. The original lights now only remain in the bays around the edge of the room, where they are supplemented by recessed down-lighters to accentuate the relief of the new wall treatment. On either side of the doors leading to the Court Suite, can be seen two of the bronze up-lighters which were formerly in the Livery Hall on the first floor.

Where once an almost unusable miscellany of furniture existed, there are now four carpeted areas furnished for sitting. All the furniture has been specially made—sofas

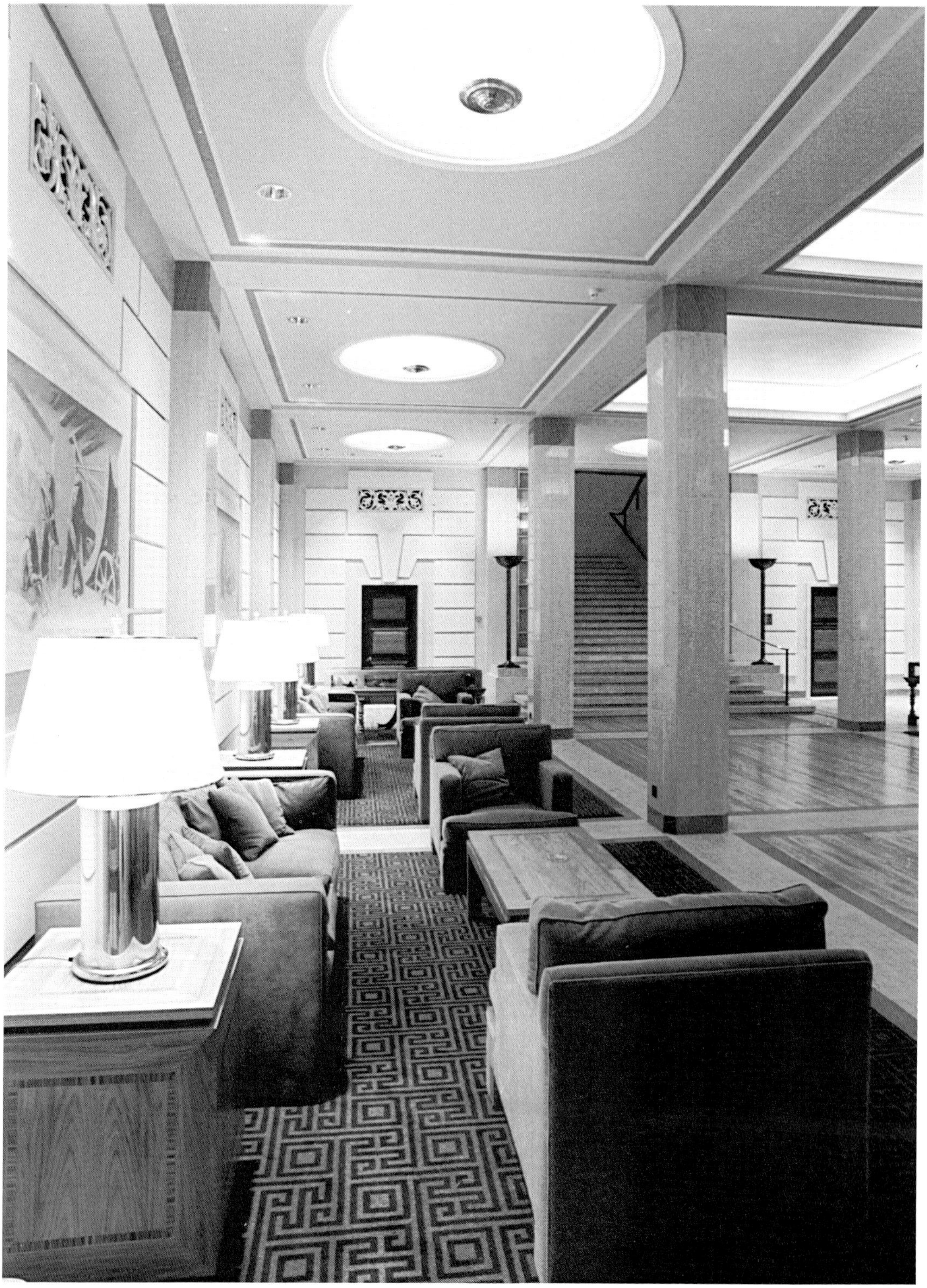

THE ENTRANCE HALL

The Entrance Hall in 1987. Where an almost unusable miscellany of furniture existed, there are now carpeted areas furnished for sitting.

One of four sitting areas in the Entrance Hall. The *trompe l'oeil* painting, which shows the process of Teaselling, is by John O'Connor.

and chairs by L.M. Kingcome Ltd. and tables in teak and African walnut by Ashby and Horner Joinery Ltd., who carried out all the joinery in the second phase of work.

A particular feature of the Entrance Hall is the set of four murals depicting the main historic processes of clothworking, the art of finishing newly woven cloth. These have been painted by John O'Connor, working through Susan Llewellyn Associates. One in each of the two centre bays of the north and south walls, the murals act as important focal points to the areas of seating and to the rusticated wall treatment generally. At the same time they introduce the visitor to the background and historical purpose of the Company. They are painted on canvas in *trompe l'oeil* to look like low-relief carvings

The Entrance Hall in 1987. The rusticated treatment of the walls is in acoustically absorbent board.

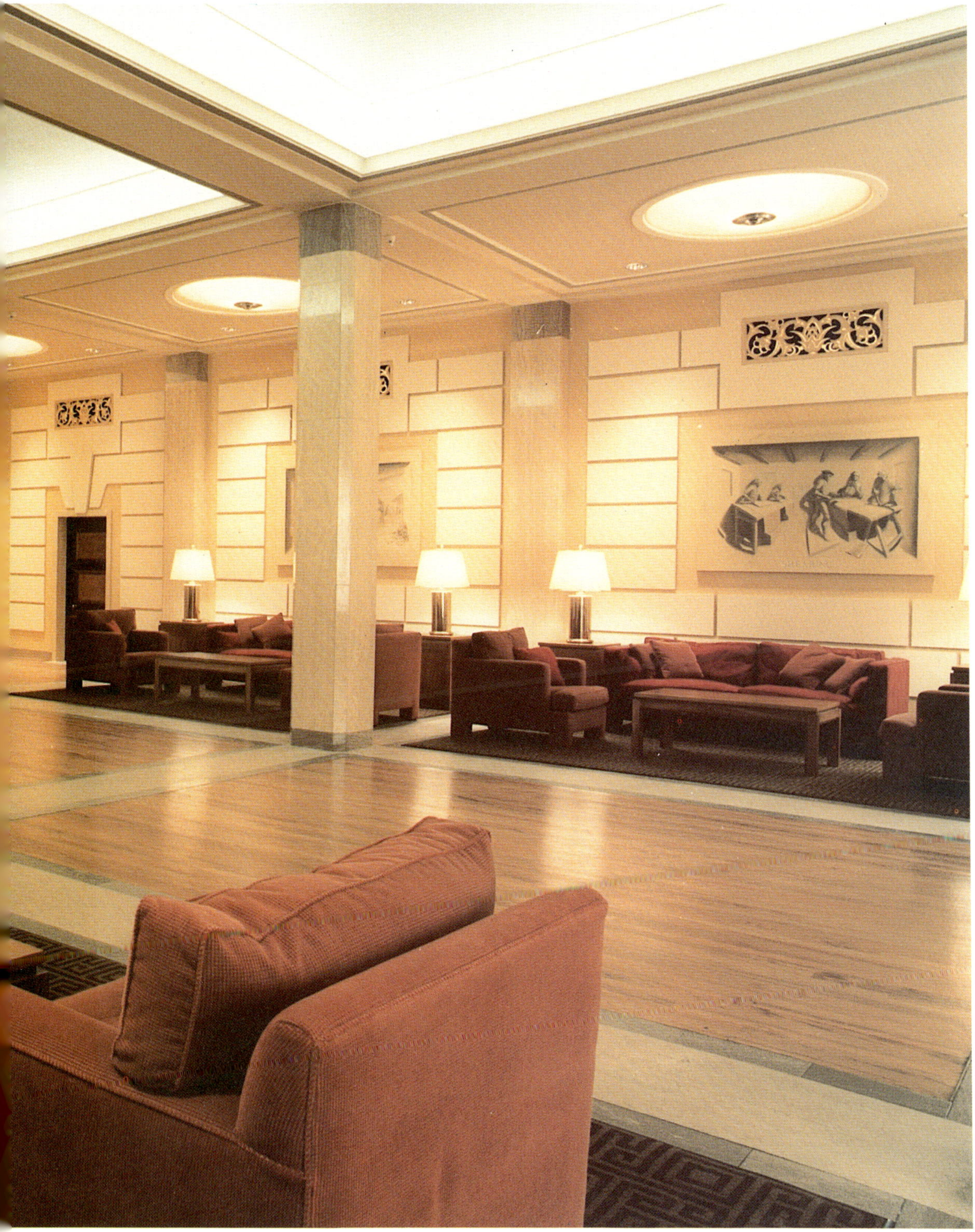

Artist's preliminary sketch in charcoal for one of the clothworking murals in the Entrance Hall.

in stone, a medium which is appropriate to their setting. With each panel illustrating a different process, the set is arranged so that, by starting on the south wall by the entrance from Dunster Court, the sequence of clothworking can be followed clockwise round the room. First comes 'Fulling' where the cloth is shown being washed in a mixture of water and fuller's earth to dissolve the grease in the wool, which is then beaten out of the fabric by the wooden hammers of the water-driven fulling mill. This process is followed by 'Tentering', during which the wet cloth is stretched on a frame to dry,

THE ENTRANCE HALL

Clay maquette of the Tentering scene made by the artist to assess the way the light would fall on the subject if carved in low relief.

Following pages: the four Entrance Hall murals by John O'Connor, illustrating the historic processes of clothworking: Fulling, Tentering, Teaselling, and Shearing.

secured there under tension by the many tenterhooks along the top and bottom rails. In this way the fabric is prevented from shrinking and dries square. It is now ready for 'Teaselling': the pieces of cloth are hung over a beam, called a perch, where labourers can work over them with teasel-heads mounted on hand-frames to raise the nap and remove loose particles of wool and other impurities. Sitting at the back of the teaselling shed in O'Connor's picture, a third labourer mounts new teasels on frames, to replace the worn ones. Outside, the teasels are being harvested in the field. Hovering frustratedly over the stony image of the cloth, is depicted the destructive Tapestry Moth, *Trichophaga*

FULLING

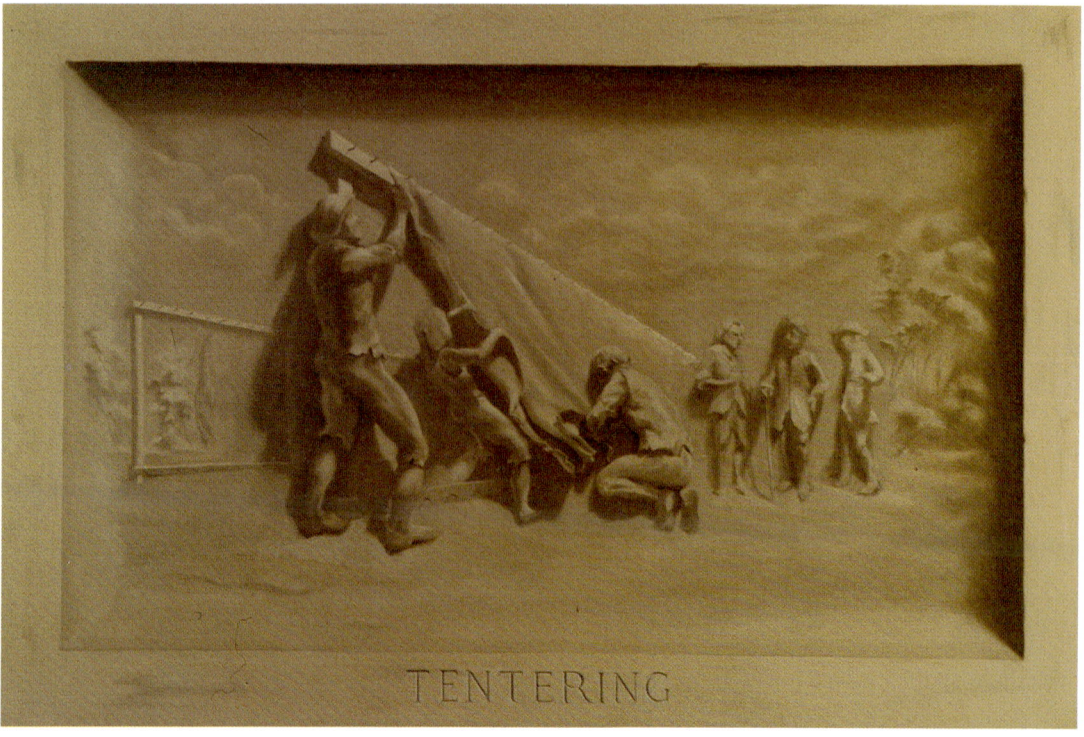

TENTERING

TEASELLING

SHEARING

Tapetzella, in its natural colours. Finally comes 'Shearing', when the cloth is laid over a padded table or horse and set by the shearmen. The pieces of cloth are held in place by double-ended hooks or habicks which secure the selvedge edge of the material to the fabric covering the table. The raised pile can then be evenly trimmed by means of broad hand-shears, held flat on the table by means of loose weights of lead held in the hand of the shearman. Alongside this process can be seen the subsequent planing of the cloth with polished blocks of wood across a sloping table to remove creases and lay flat what is left of the pile. In this final scene the artist is depicted brushing up the sheared wool into a small pan. His bill has been allowed to fall to the floor and on it can be seen his signature.

The subjects of the murals were drawn from illustrated books and engravings in the Company's possession. Preliminary sketches in charcoal were first prepared by the artist and developed in collaboration with Thomas Girtin, past Master, and the Company's Archivist, David Wickham, to ensure their authenticity. Then, to determine how the light would fall on the subject if it were really carved in stone (different of course, because of the low relief, from real life), clay maquettes were made and lit from the appropriate angle. At this point work on the actual paintings could be started, with the subject first sketched in lightly with charcoal and then built up in a series of semi-transparent glazes to simulate three dimensions.

A feature of the Entrance Hall, as originally built, was the series of glazed screens and doors with frames in silver-bronze. A further set of matching sliding doors has been made by Pollards of London Ltd. for the opening at the foot of the Grand Staircase. These not only help to dress what was once a rather stark opening but, by providing a barrier between the Entrance Hall and the Ceremonial Rooms on the floor above, they give greater scope for the independent use of the Entrance Hall for special events and even exhibitions.

Leading directly from the Hall are two sets of cloakrooms. As part of the first phase of work, the Gentlemen's Cloakroom was completely reorganised and re-fitted with a new coat-hanging system. This provides not only enough hooks to cope with big dinner nights, but also separate hangers in an area adjacent to the Court Corridor for use by members of the Court when the Cloakroom is unattended. The design also incorporates a telephone booth, pigeon-holes for Court mail and papers, and shelving for

The Gentlemen's Cloakroom before refurbishment.

The Cloakroom after refurbishment.

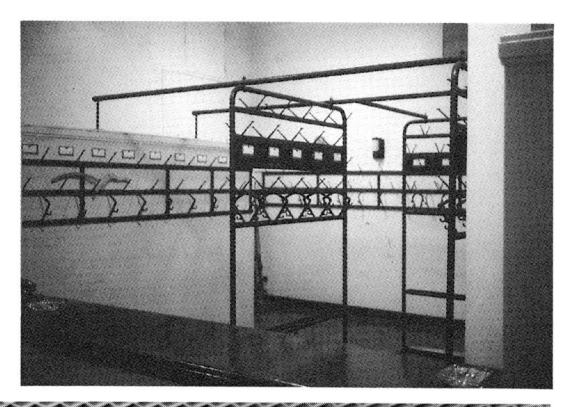

THE CRAFTSMAN IN THE CITY

The Entrance Hall looking east towards the entrance to the Court Suite.

New sliding glazed doors in silver-bronze frames at the foot of the Grand Staircase. The design matches those installed in the 1950s elsewhere in the room.

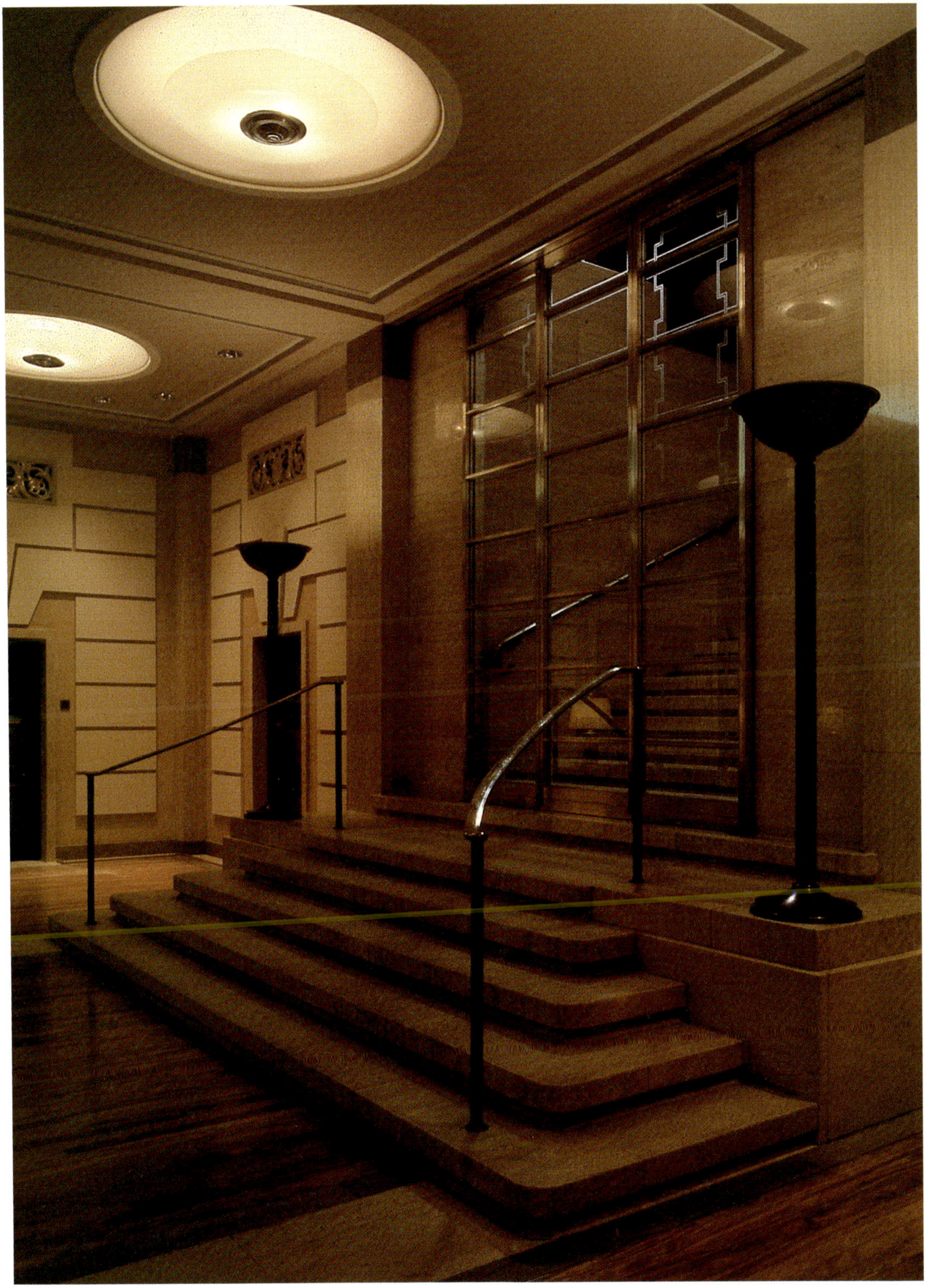

suitcases. The suspended ceiling allows space above for pipes and ductwork. A similar exercise in the second phase was carried out in the Ladies' Cloakroom. Here four changing cubicles have been provided in much the same manner as those created for members of the Livery. New joinery throughout this Cloakroom is in teak, to match the Entrance Hall.

IV The Court Suite

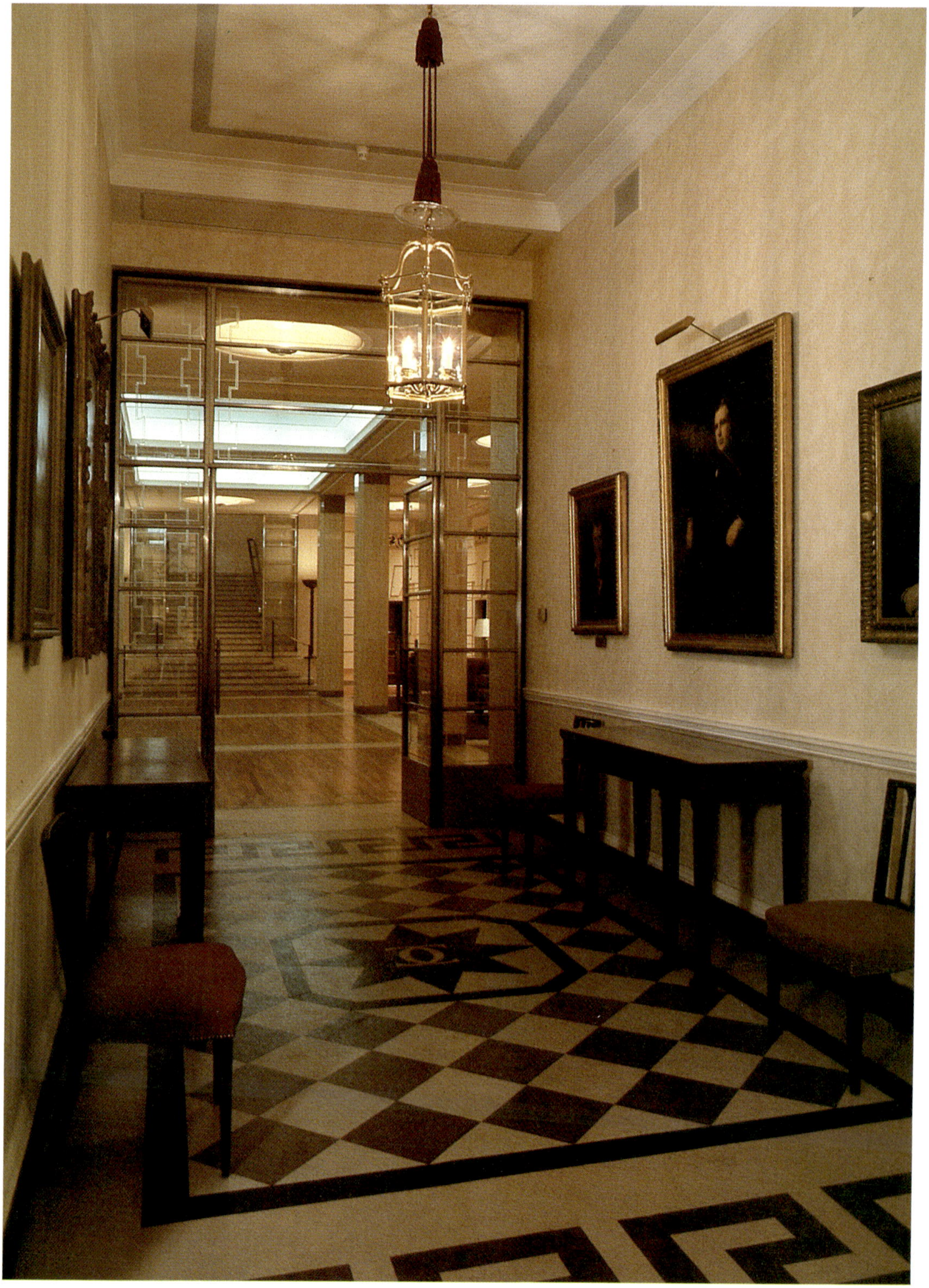

THE COURT SUITE

The Court Corridor looking towards the Entrance Hall after refurbishment. A new linoleum floor replaces the cork laid in the 1950s.

Below: laying the new floor in the Corridor.

The Court Suite is on the ground floor at the east end of the building. This is the semi-private part of the Hall where the Court and committees meet to determine the Company's business, the modern day equivalent of the Parlour of earlier Halls. It comprises three rooms: the Court Drawing Room, the Court Luncheon Room and the Court Room, each of which leads off the Court Corridor. Work on this part of the Hall was carried out during 1985.

The relationship of the Court Corridor to the Entrance Hall is important, for not only does it lead directly from it, but it terminates the principal architectural axis which runs through the building. Colours here have been left neutral to harmonise with the Hall and maintain the sense, if not the reality, of the marble within that space. The scheme gives a further unifying effect to the architecture of the Corridor itself, where before the contrasting tones of dado, upper wall and ceiling had tended to divide it horizontally into layers. To improve the proportions of the space, friezes and cornices have been added above the architraves to the doors; these had been intended when the Hall was designed, but were never installed. A feature of the Corridor is the new floor which replaces the cork laid down in the 1950s and which had become extremely worn. The new floor finish is traditional linoleum, laid by one man who was responsible for setting it out on site and for cutting the thousands of pieces that make up the design.

THE CRAFTSMAN IN THE CITY

The Court Corridor looking south
before refurbishment.

THE COURT SUITE

A new brass lantern in the Court Corridor.

One of the ramshead mounts which adorn the new lanterns.

In the centre of each bay, the crossed 'C's of The Clothworkers' Company are set in an eight-pointed star.

A major addition to this space is the large display cabinet, built in Brazilian mahogany by Elliotts of Reading, who carried out all the joinery in the first phase of work. It was designed in the manner of Thomas Chippendale specially for this position where it can be seen from the Entrance Hall; inside is a collection of armorial china commissioned by the Company from the Spode factory. Five new brass and glass lanterns hang

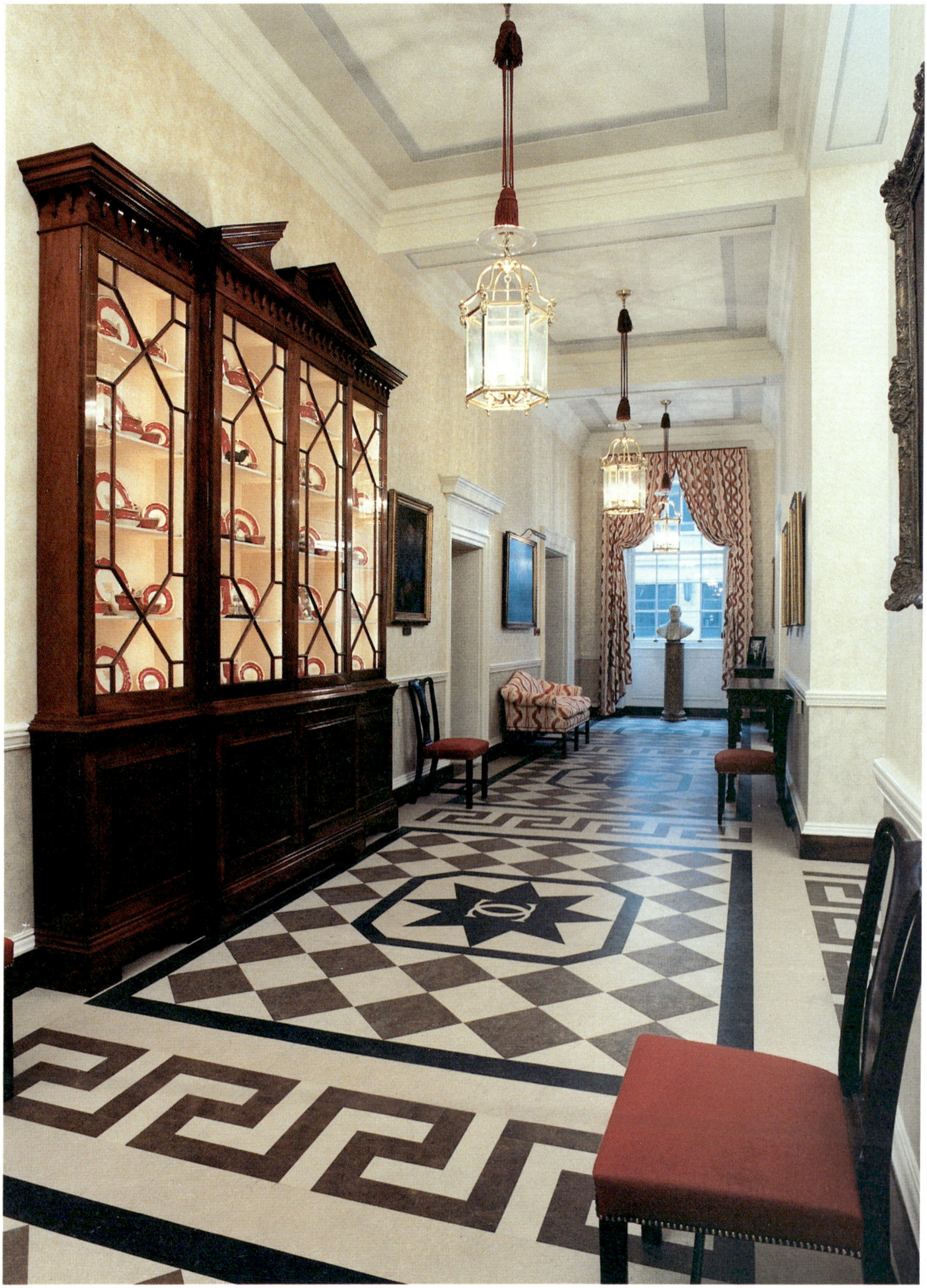

THE COURT SUITE

The Court Corridor looking south in 1986 after refurbishment.

A detail of the new display cabinet made by Elliotts of Reading. It contains a collection of armorial china commissioned by The Clothworkers' Company from the Spode factory.

67

THE CRAFTSMAN IN THE CITY

Left: after alternative means of support had been provided, cutting out the original structural stanchion to make way for the new doors into the Drawing Room.

Right: the new steel 'H' frame complete and ready for the installation of wall and door linings.

from the Corridor ceiling. They are basically a standard design, to which have been added ramshead mounts and glass smoke-dishes, which in the eighteenth century would have prevented the burning candles from depositing soot on the ceiling. The method of hanging the lanterns by ropes and tassels also derives from the eighteenth century, when it would have been necessary to lower and raise the lanterns to light the candles; the tassels would then have hidden the pulley-blocks and counter-weights.

The principal architectural change to the Court Corridor has been the provision of new double doors leading to the Drawing Room. Formerly access to this room had been provided through two single doors, which made the arrangement of furniture within the room extremely awkward. It had originally been intended for committees,

THE COURT SUITE

The Court Corridor looking north. The new doors to the Drawing Room are on the left.

and although subsequently used as a drawing room, it was never properly furnished as one. A pair of central doors were therefore introduced to improve the plan of the room and provide less restricted passage to and from the Corridor, an important consideration when the room is being used by thirty or so members of the Company before a Court meeting or a Freedom ceremony. There were, in fact, good structural reasons for the original arrangement of two doors, since passing through the centre of the open-

70

THE COURT SUITE

Left above: the Court Drawing Room before refurbishment. The two single doors gave on to the Court Corridor.

Below: the Drawing Room after refurbishment, showing the new doors and marble chimneypiece of mid-eighteenth century design.

Festoon curtains in the Court Drawing Room.

ing which it was now intended to create was one of the main structural stanchions of the building. Investigations by the structural engineer revealed, however, that it was quite possible to modify the steel frame so that the relevant part of the stanchion could be removed. The decision was therefore taken to go ahead. The adopted scheme involved inserting on either side of the original stanchion additional stanchions through which the loads from above would be transferred to new reinforced beams in the floor below. The critical section of the original could then be cut away. This was a somewhat hair-raising process to watch, despite the engineer's calculations which intimated that all

THE CRAFTSMAN IN THE CITY

Security shutter built into a new window lining in the Court Drawing Room.

Design for a girandole from the third edition of Thomas Chippendale's *Gentleman and Cabinet-Maker's Director*, 1762.

would be well! The structural opening having been achieved, the linings could then be built-up and new polished mahogany doors hung to match the others in the Corridor.

It seemed that each of the principal rooms had an individual and recognisable character which it was felt could be related directly to an historic period or style. In some cases it was more obvious than in others. The Drawing Room seemed to belong to the third quarter of the eighteenth century, a time when decoration was greatly influenced by Thomas Chippendale's *Gentleman and Cabinet-Maker's Director*. The decision to follow this period was perhaps further influenced by the fact that the Company already owned a large *Italian Landscape* after Claude Lorrain and a fine giltwood Chinese Chippendale looking-glass, both of which would hang well in the room. To strengthen the sense of period, a marble chimneypiece of mid-eighteenth century design was bought from Crowther of Syon Lodge and fitted into what was once an alcove, but which has now

THE COURT SUITE

Working up a clay model of one of the new Drawing Room girandoles from a full size drawing in order to agree the design in detail before carving in wood.

Clay model. The carved hoho bird replaces the carved urn of Chippendale's design.

been filled in to create a chimney breast. On the walls is a green verditer paper by Zoffany Ltd., copied from an eighteenth century fragment at Temple Newsam near Leeds and finished with a giltwood strip around the edge. The Turkey patterned carpet, a feature fashionable at that time, was woven specially. The mid-eighteenth century was also the period for festoon and reefed curtains of silk damask, which drew up rather than across, and it seemed fitting to adopt this approach here where the windows are tall and where maximum light at low level is desirable. As in all the principal rooms now, the window reveals have been given panelled linings and architraves, which are here shown off to good advantage. Entirely modern, but discreet, additions are the metal security shutters, which have been built into the new linings of all the ground floor windows. Operated by electrical motors, they roll up to the top of the windows out of sight behind the curtain valances when the rooms are being used.

THE CRAFTSMAN IN THE CITY

Final touches to the gilding of the new girandoles in the carver's workshop.

One of the girandoles made for the Court Drawing Room by Anthony Harrington.

For lighting in the Drawing Room, Thomas Chippendale was again consulted. A set of four carved and gilt girandoles has been made for the room by Anthony Harrington. Their design is based on a plate in Chippendale's *Director*, though the proportions have been slightly adjusted to suit their location, and the rather pedestrian urn of the original design has been replaced by the more interesting and sinuous hoho bird. In order to get the design right in the third dimension, a full-size model in clay was made, examined, altered and developed until it felt right, after which carving could

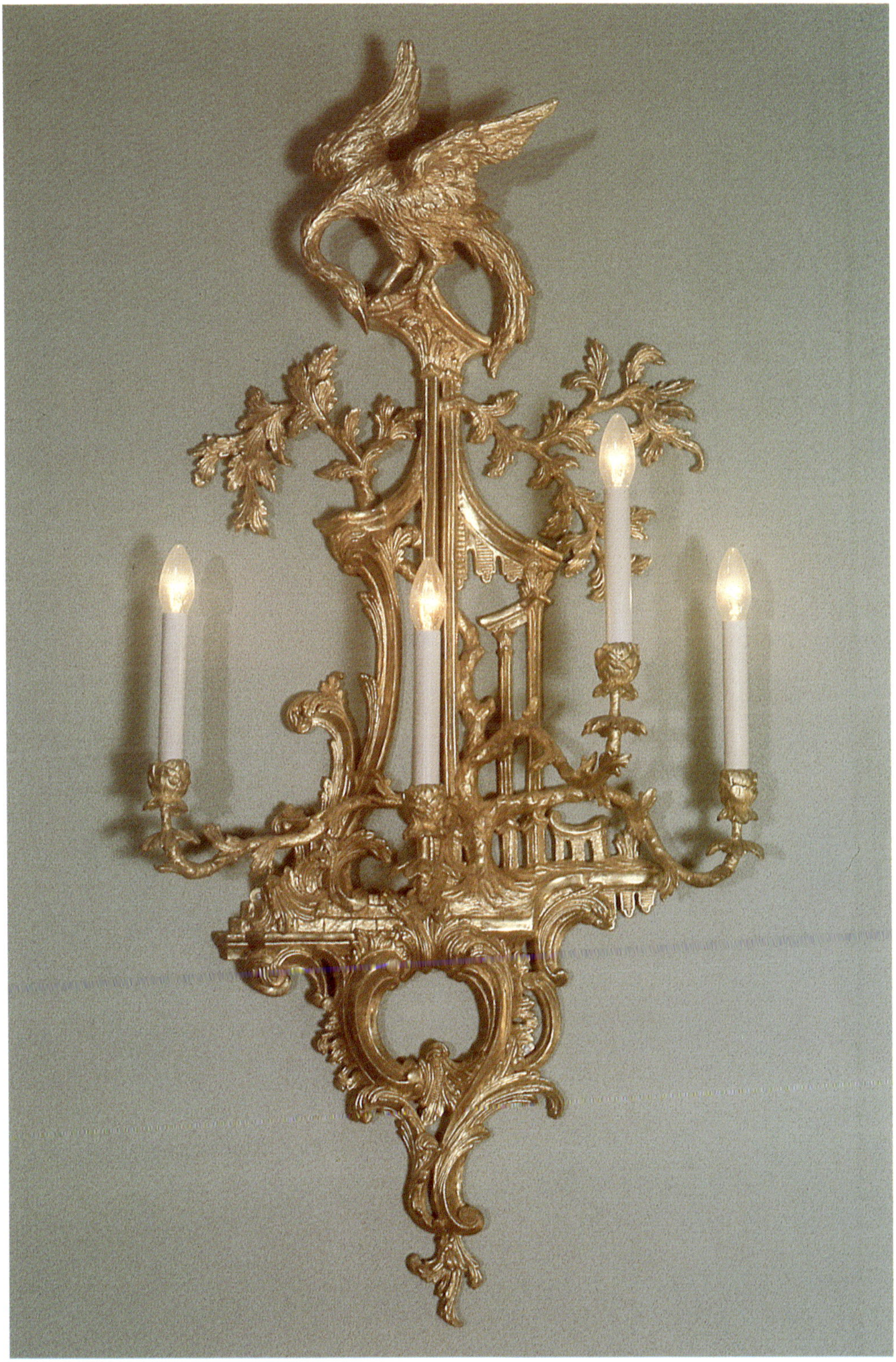

THE CRAFTSMAN IN THE CITY

Nineteenth century chandelier in the Court Luncheon Room.

One of a pair of gilt-metal wall brackets in the same room.

The Court Luncheon Room after refurbishment, with tables laid for a Ladies' Dinner.

start. The final detail and the positions of the arms were left until the main carving was sufficiently advanced to be looked at in position on site. The brackets were then taken back to the carver's workshop in Kent, where they were finished and gilded.

New light fittings have been something of a feature of the refurbishment. Generally because of the need to provide sets of fittings, they have been specially made, but in the Court Luncheon Room where a single chandelier and a pair of brackets only were required, it was possible to find fittings that already existed. The Luncheon Room

77

THE CRAFTSMAN IN THE CITY

One of the new Court Luncheon Room tables made by Elliotts of Reading. The form of the pedestal was inspired by the clothworker's habick.

Above: the Court Luncheon Room before refurbishment.

Below: the Court Luncheon Room after refurbishment. A new pair of pilasters with a beam between them have been built to balance a similar arrangement existing at the west end of the room. The new beam contains a ventilation duct which has made possible the removal of unsightly grilles from the upper walls.

chandelier is in the style of the Regency period, though it was probably built in the mid-nineteenth century; it is known because of its shape as a 'lighthouse' chandelier. The gilt-metal of the arms is matched in the two wall brackets. They suit the essentially early-nineteenth century character which this room seemed to have; and this has been reinforced by the new decorations. The colour scheme has been devised to take account of the blue leather chairs which form part of the large Livery Hall suite made for the Company in the 1950s and which was to be retained. The set of tables is a new addition to the room. Built on central pedestals whose design is derived from the clothworking habick, these can be set together in a variety of arrangements to suit different occasions. The edges of the tops are rebated to take brass tongues which hold the tables together and keep them level where they butt one against another. In this way it is possible to sit comfortably at any point along a made-up length.

Changes have also been made to the architecture of this room. As elsewhere, the

THE COURT SUITE

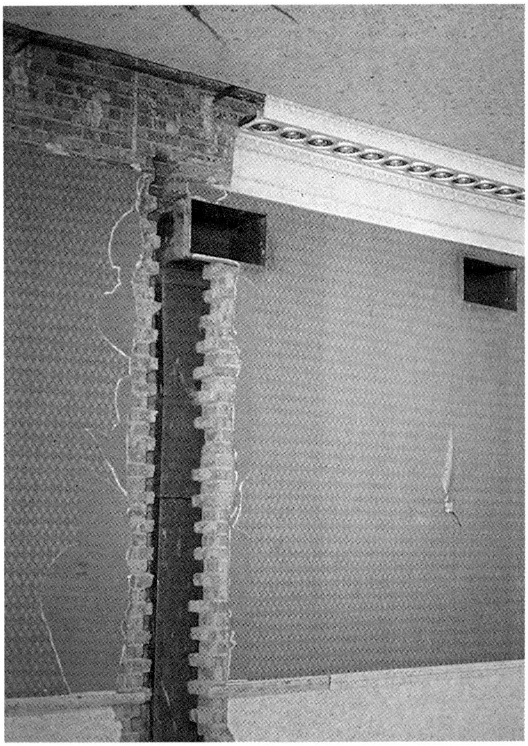

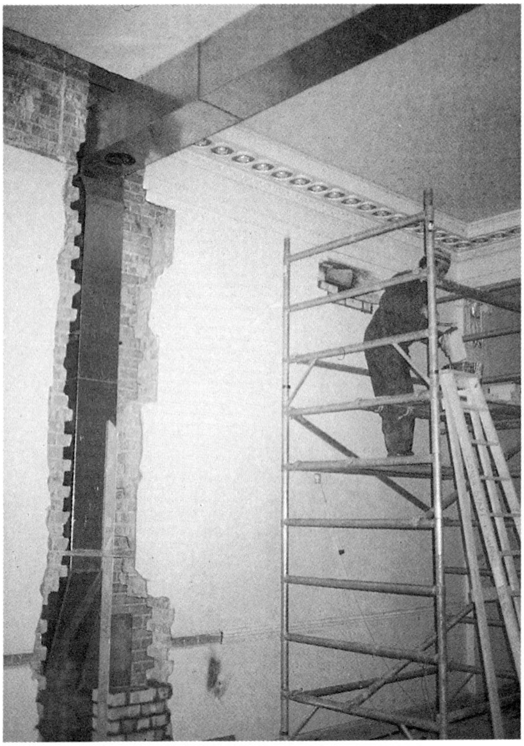

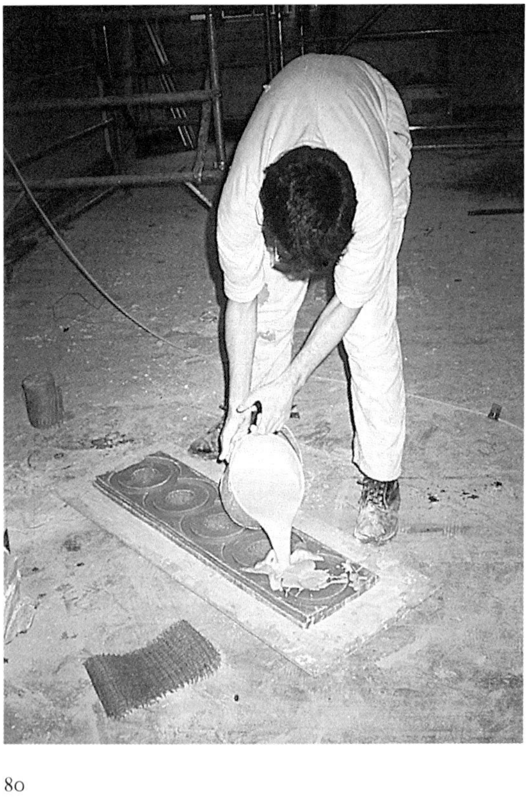

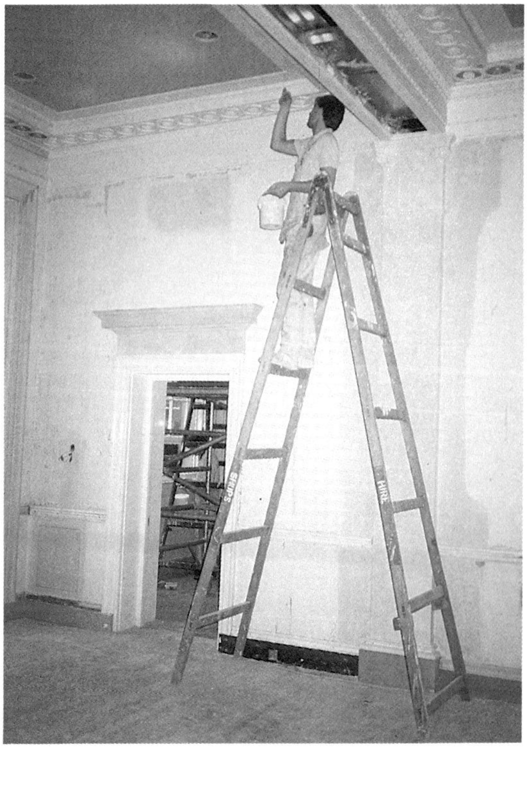

Wall in the Court Luncheon Room opened to reveal a vertical duct serving high level ventilation grilles.

The new horizontal duct which carries fresh air across the room.

Casting part of a new fibrous plaster cornice in a flexible mould taken from an existing detail in the room.

Fixing the plaster 'beam casing' around the new ventilation duct.

Following pages: Carpet making at Woodward Grosvenor and Company's factory:
The wool being dyed.
The dyed wool being wound on to bobbins ready for transfer to the loom.
The wool being drawn off the bobbins onto the loom.
The border of the Court Luncheon Room carpet on the loom, watched by Lieutenant-Commander and Mrs Peter Angell.

windows now have linings and the curtains have been brought out on to the face of the wall. Like the Court Corridor the doorcases have been given friezes and cornices. More significantly, the unsightly ventilation grilles, which formerly disfigured the upper walls of the room, have gone; and the pilasters and beam at the back of the room have been balanced by a second set in a corresponding position at the opposite end of the room. The two changes were not unconnected. Records showed that the grilles all supplied air to the room from a single vertical duct which rose in the thickness of the wall. It was feasible to divert the supply and re-route it through a new duct which spanned the width of the room in a position corresponding to the structural beam already in place at the other end. By inserting grilles in the underside of the new duct and encasing it in plaster to match the existing beam, the visual impact of the ventilation system has been minimised and the architectural balance of the room improved. Originally the shafts of the supporting pilasters had been left white, but it was felt that, now they had become such a feature of the room, a bolder approach might look better. They have therefore been finished to simulate marble, a fascinating process to watch and achieved in a single coat by working over a coloured glaze with brushes, feathers and cloths.

The carpets in all the principal rooms were made of worsted Wilton in Kidderminster by Woodward Grosvenor and Company Ltd., and then fitted by Albany Carpets Ltd. The Luncheon Room carpet, like most that have now been laid, is made up of a body in one design framed with a separate border in a different but co-ordinated design, giving the effect of a single woven rug made to fit the room. All the carpets were in fact woven in strips either twenty-seven or thirty-six inches wide and then sewn together. Most of the body designs were selected from existing patterns, but the borders were specially designed. Special colours were selected to suit the different rooms: in the case of the Luncheon Room it was only after several dyeing trials that a blue which would go with the chairs was achieved.

The process of carpet-making was of special interest to the Company with its traditions in the wool trade; and a party comprising Lieutenant-Commander Peter Angell, past Master, and his wife, with the Assistant Clerk and the author, went up to Kidderminster to see some of the new carpets going through various stages of manufacture, from dyeing the wool to final hand-finishing after the carpet had come off the loom.

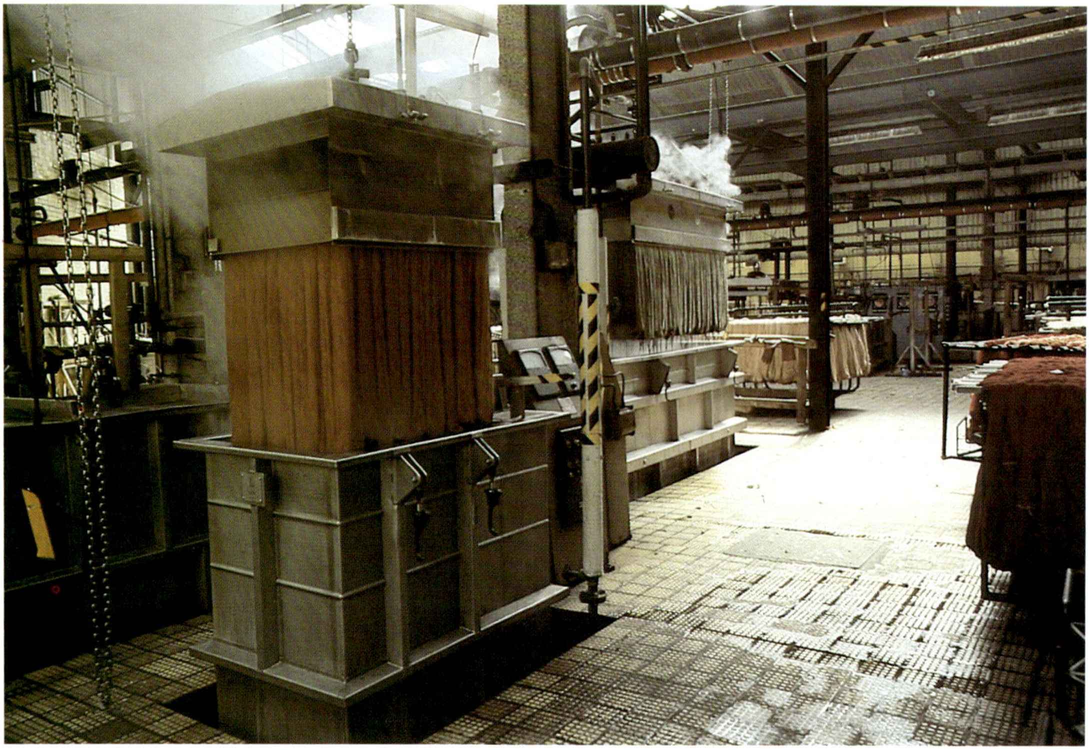

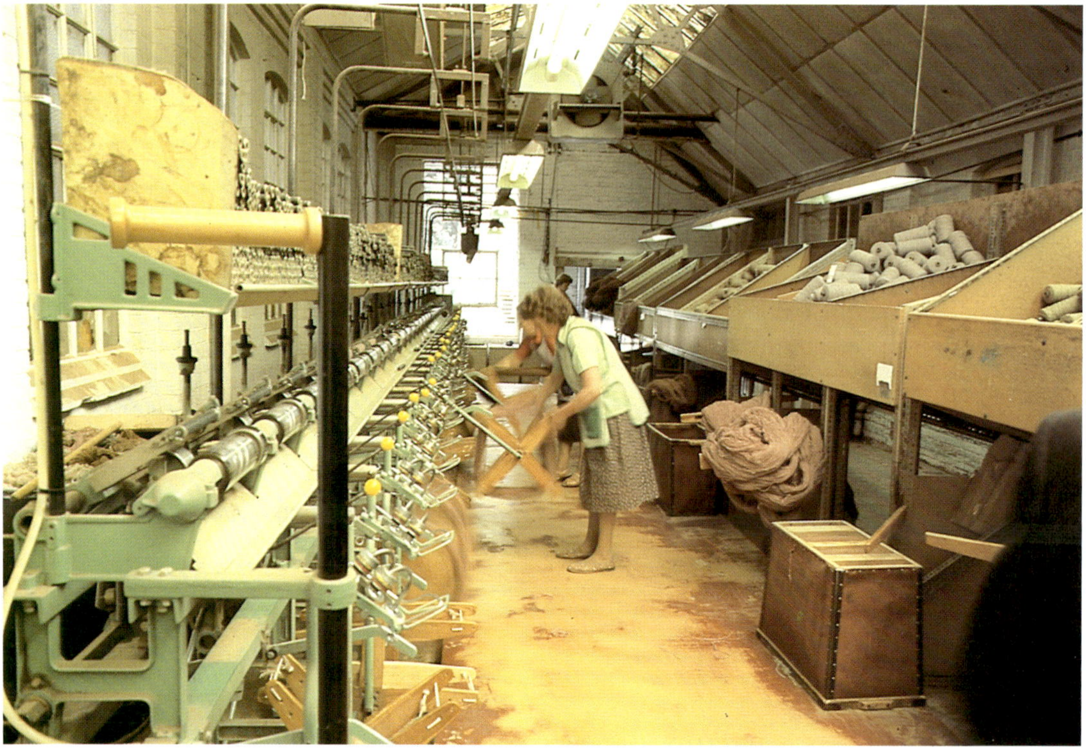

83

THE CRAFTSMAN IN THE CITY

Left: length of carpet for the Court Room, at the factory.

Right: the same carpet laid in the Court Room at Clothworkers' Hall.

Above: the Court Room before refurbishment.

Below: the Court Room after refurbishment.

One of the carpets to find most favour has been that in the Court Room. The thirty-six inch widths, when joined together, form a magnificent pattern and the soft colours of pink and three greens provide an excellent background for the existing chairs and new curtains in this room. The Court Room had always been a handsome, well-lit and well-proportioned space, and it has been changed perhaps less than most. Overdoors have, however, been added as elsewhere in the Court Suite, and the window reveals have been lined and fitted with security shutters. The room has been decorated, using

85

The Court Room in 1987.

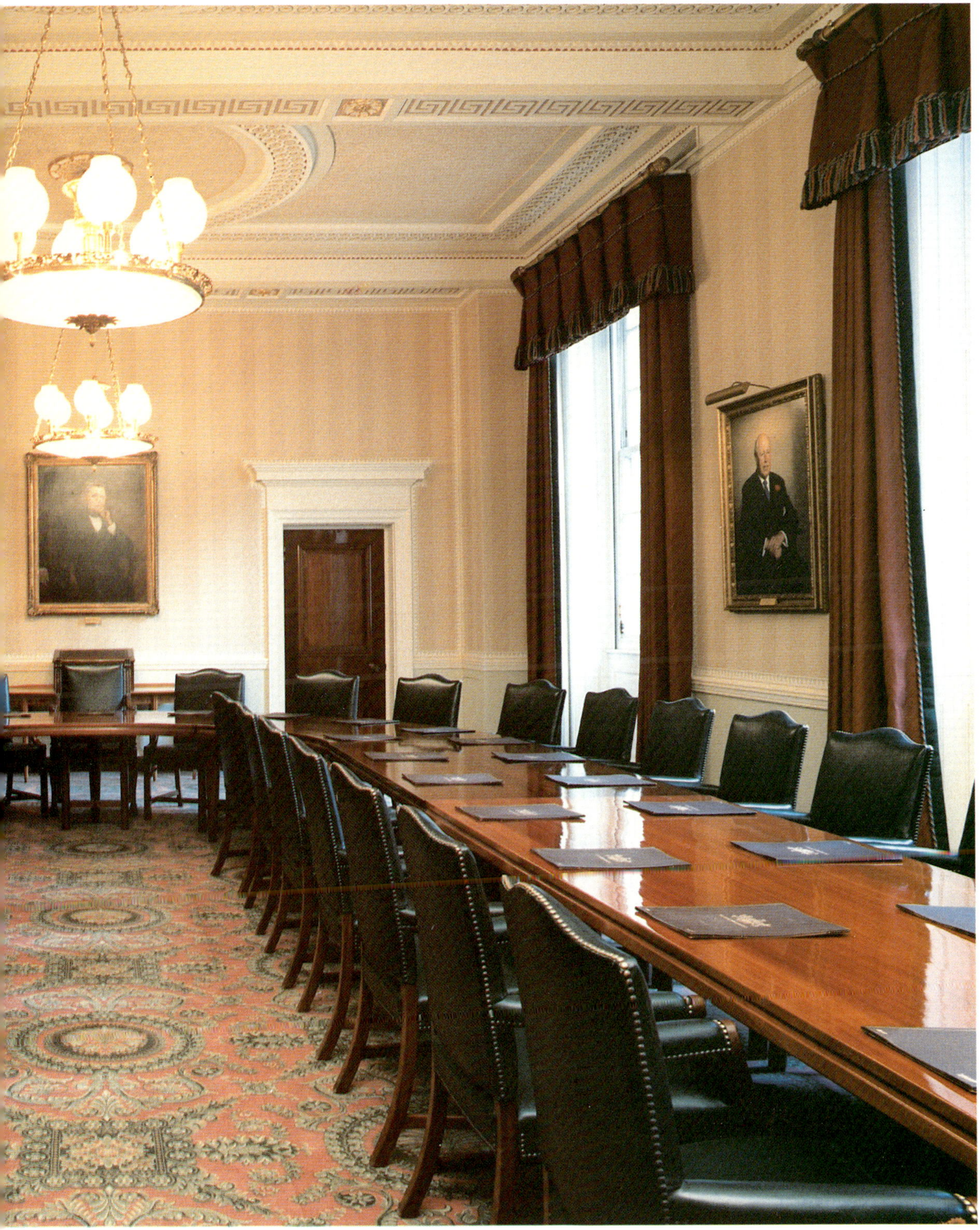

The cut-glass dish of one of the Court Room light-fittings.

Right: a Court Room light-fitting, based on an early-nineteenth century colza oil lamp.

striped paper with borders for the walls, where previously there had been emulsion. As in a number of other rooms, the original hair-mat acoustic lining to the ceiling has been replaced by sprayed acoustic plaster.

Specially made light-fittings replace those installed in the 1950s. Like the Luncheon Room, the Court Room has an early-nineteenth century feel and the design of the light-

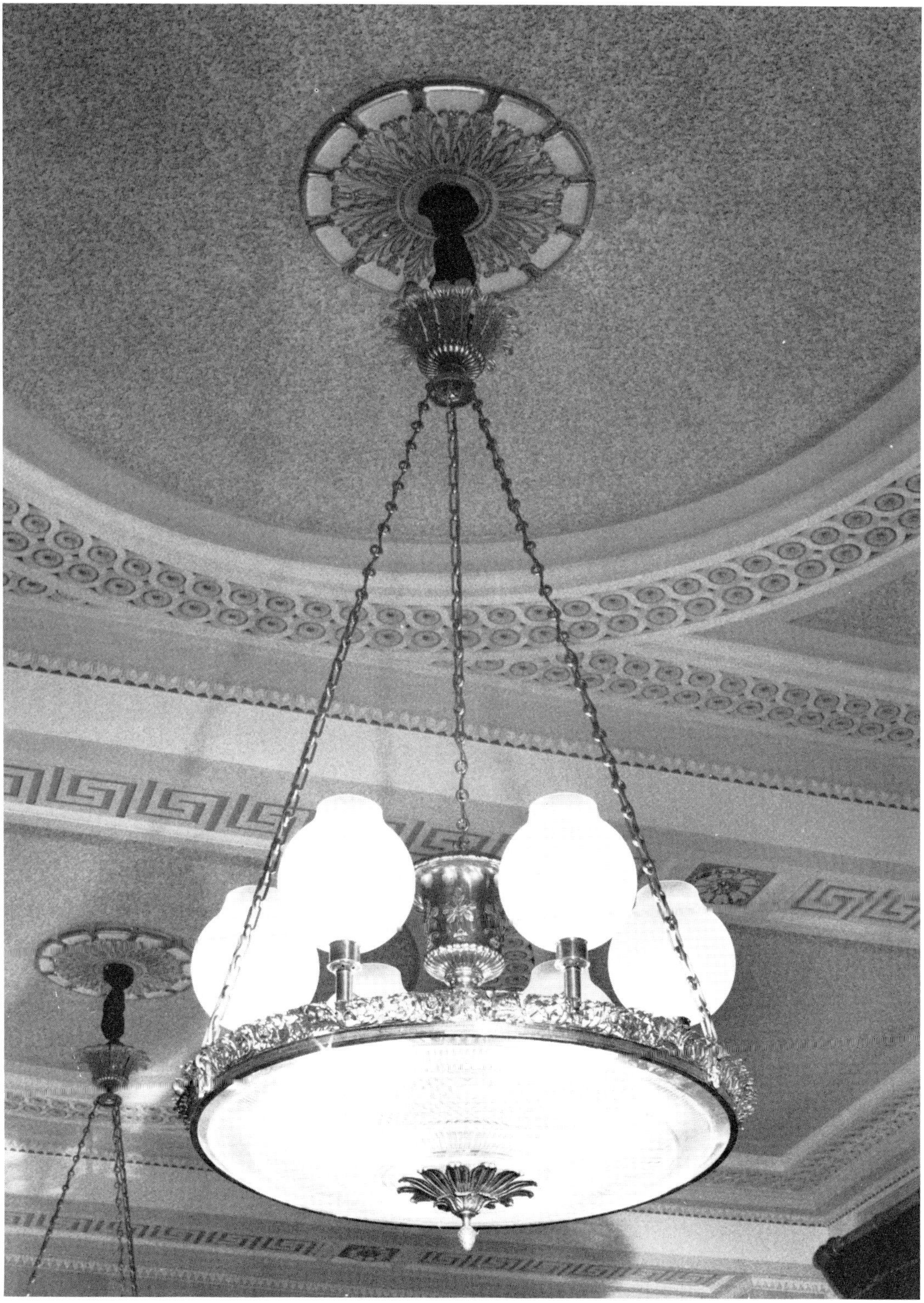

fittings here is appropriate to this. It derives from early colza oil lamps: instead of candles these burned a heavy oil, which was stored in a central reservoir, often designed as a classical urn. The oil was then fed downwards through metal tubes to a circuit of shaded burners arranged around the perimeter of the fitting. Suspended below the burners would have been a finely cut glass dish, shown off to advantage by the light which shone through it. For the Court Room, essentially a working room in which papers have to be read, such a fitting, adapted for electricity, has great practical advantages for, in addition to the lamps in the burners, it has been possible to conceal a network of twelve 100 watt bulbs immediately above the dish. Thus these fittings are capable of great output within the framework of a traditional design. Like all the lighting in the main rooms they can also be dimmed to provide the most suitable level of light for whatever way the space may be used. The fittings were made by R. Wilkinson and Son in south London. The metalwork was cast from original models in brass and then gilded. The glass of the dishes is in fact German spectacle glass, which arrived in England flat. Dishing was achieved by heating the glass to softening temperature, at which point the necessary curve could be achieved by laying the glass over an appropriate mould. Each dish is thirty-three inches across, as large as is practicable for one man to hold against the cutting wheel. Uncut, each dish weighed forty pounds, and of this some seven pounds of glass was cut away to provide the sparkling pattern. A single dish took four weeks to cut.

With the refurbishment of the Court Suite completed as part of the first phase of work, members of the Company were able to see some results before embarking on the major spaces at first floor level. Happily reactions were favourable, and the project moved on to tackle the main Ceremonial Rooms and the Livery Hall itself.

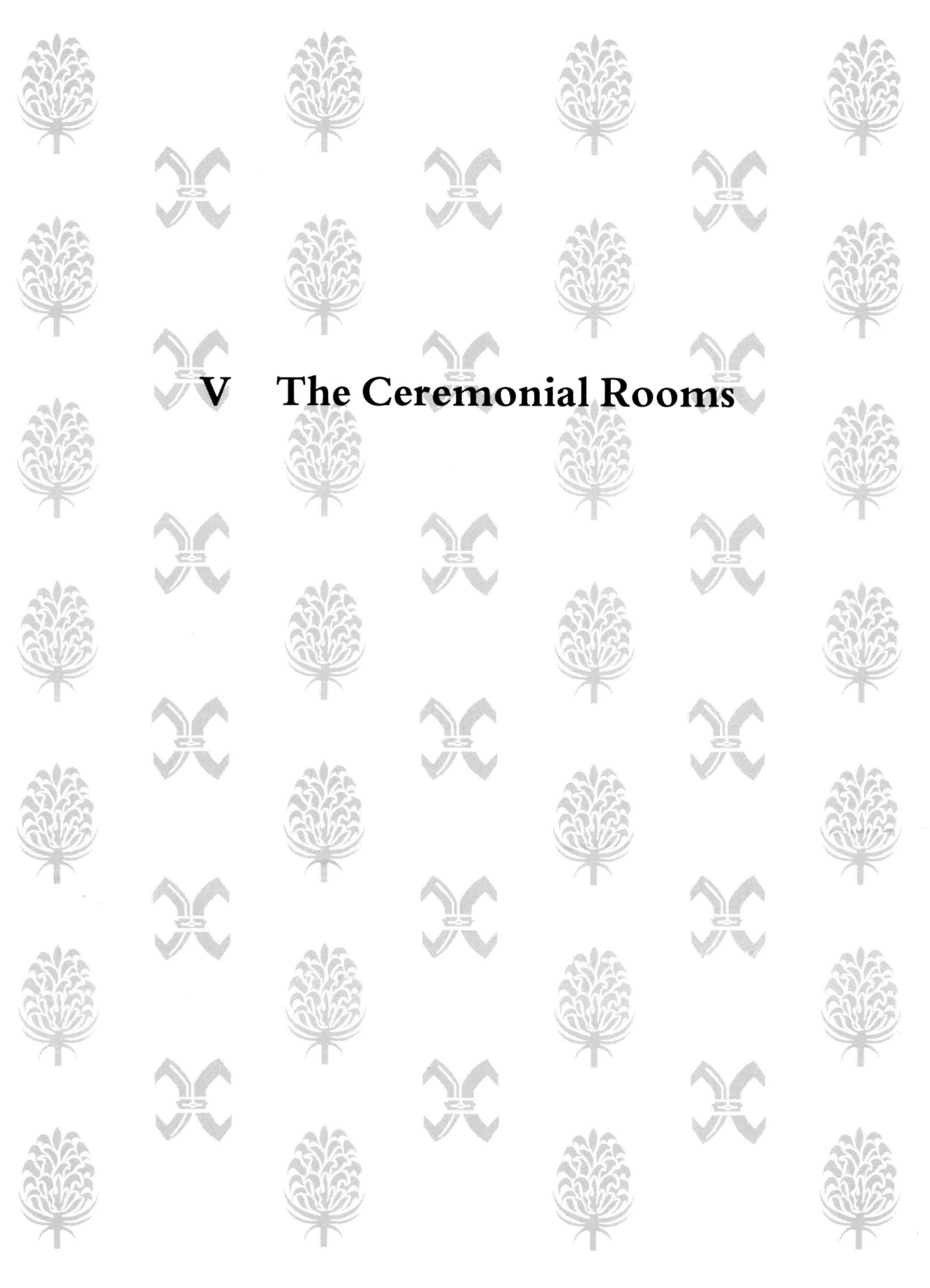

V The Ceremonial Rooms

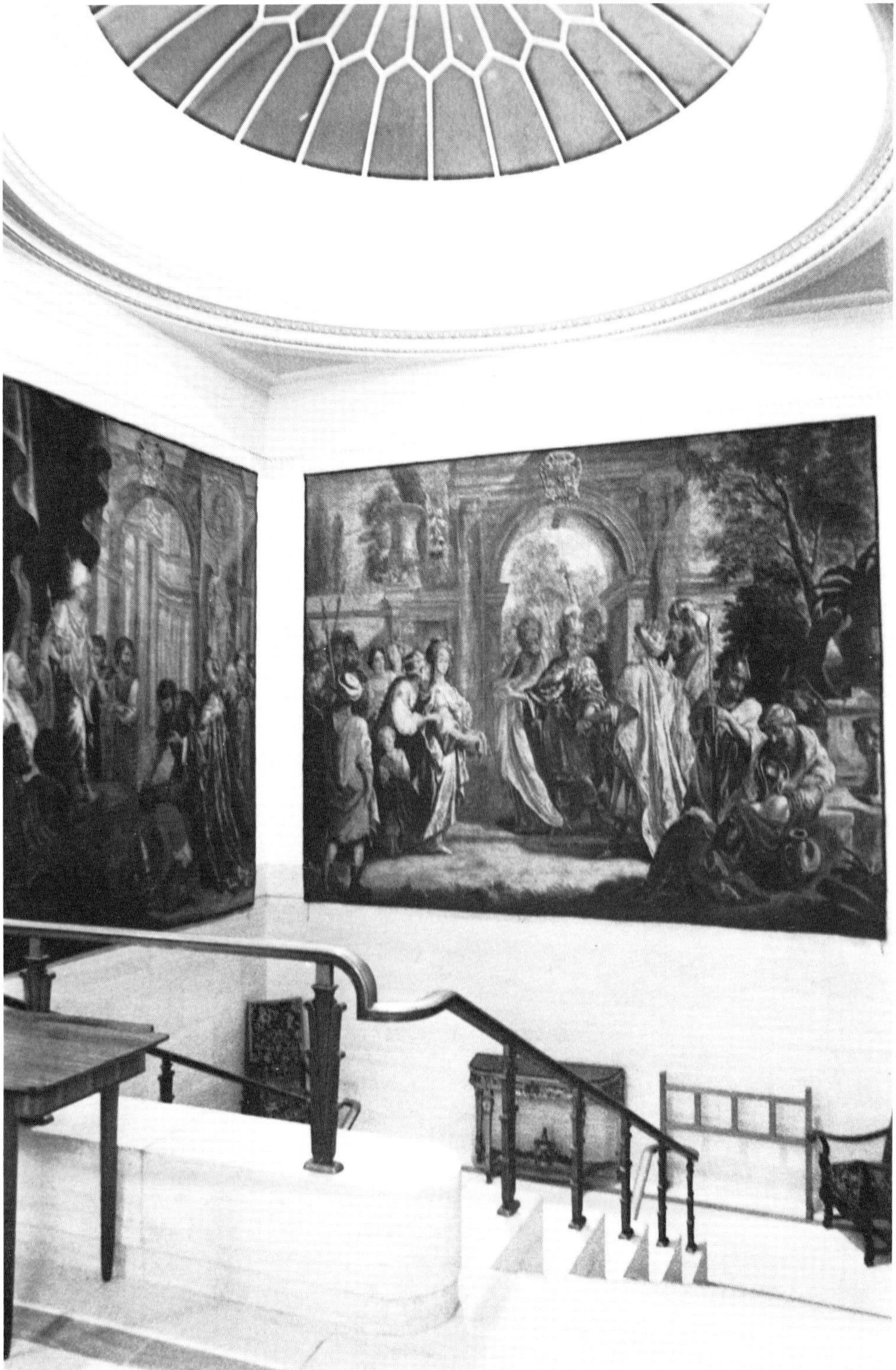

THE CEREMONIAL ROOMS

The Grand Staircase before refurbishment. Daylight coming through the glazed dome was blocked out to protect the tapestries purchased by the Company in 1970.

The Reception Landing, the Reception Room, the Library and the Livery Hall form the principal suite of rooms for public entertaining on the first floor. They are approached by way of the Grand Staircase from the west end of the Entrance Hall. On the Staircase are to be found three magnificent tapestries purchased by the Company in 1970. They were made in Brussels between 1771 and 1775 for the Empress Maria Theresa, and they depict scenes from the story of Cyrus the Great, founder of the Persian empire. The fine colours have survived naturally without being brightened with paint, an expedient often resorted to when fading has occurred. To maintain this condition, it had been necessary for the Company to black-out the formerly naturally-lit dome above. Whilst protecting the tapestries, this did little for the appearance of the dome. It has now been possible to restore the original effect without placing the tapestries at risk, by means of introducing diffused artificial lighting above the inner skin of glazing. The dome has been further embellished by gilding the ribs supporting the glazing and by decorating the plaster band above the cornice with a frieze of habicks and teasels.

On the half-landing stands a new table of travertine marble; it incorporates a panel made up of sections of carved and gilded fretwork displaying the cyphers of the Company's first royal Freeman, James I, and of his son Charles I. These are survivals from the fourth Hall of c. 1668 where they were mounted in the panelling of the Livery Hall above the statues of the monarchs.

In 1968, the year he became Master, Cedric Morgan presented the Company with a magnificent three-quarter life-size gilded model of a Dorset Horn Ram. It was carved from Japanese oak by Jack Denny, a master tailor from Southwold in Suffolk. It is now displayed with considerable dignity in a specially designed niche on the landing at the top of the stair, where it can be seen by visitors as they approach the Ceremonial Rooms. The plinth and classical surround in travertine marble were executed by Albion Stone Masonry Ltd., who also built the table and carried out all the marble cleaning and alteration during the project.

The Grand Staircase has been redecorated to a new colour scheme, the rich *lapis lazuli* blue of the columns and pilasters supporting the strong colours of the tapestries and introducing a blue theme which runs through the whole suite of main rooms and which is designed to support the continued use of the Livery Hall chairs. Many of the architectural enrichments here had been gilded in the late 1960s, and it has been possible by

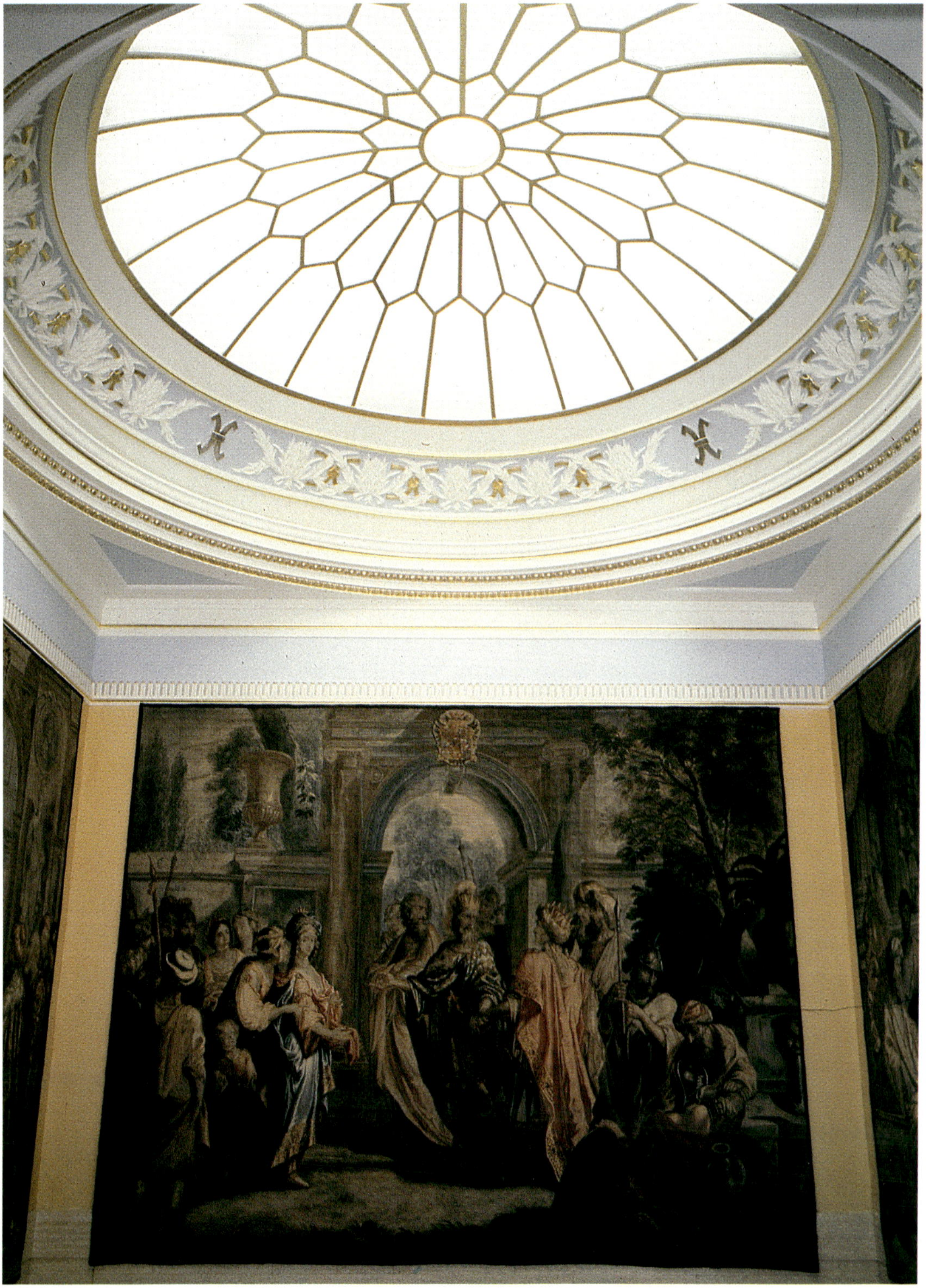

THE CEREMONIAL ROOMS

The Grand Staircase after refurbishment. Artificial lighting above the dome has restored the originally intended effect without threat to the tapestries.

The glazed dome, embellished with a new frieze of habicks and teasels.

95

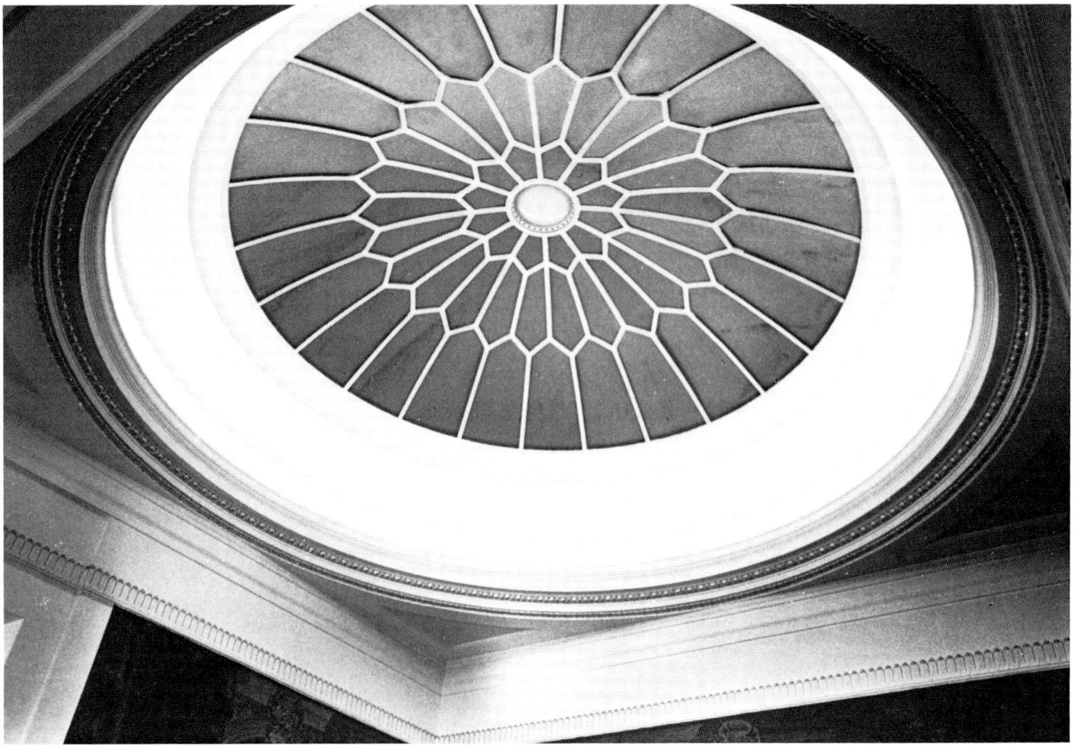

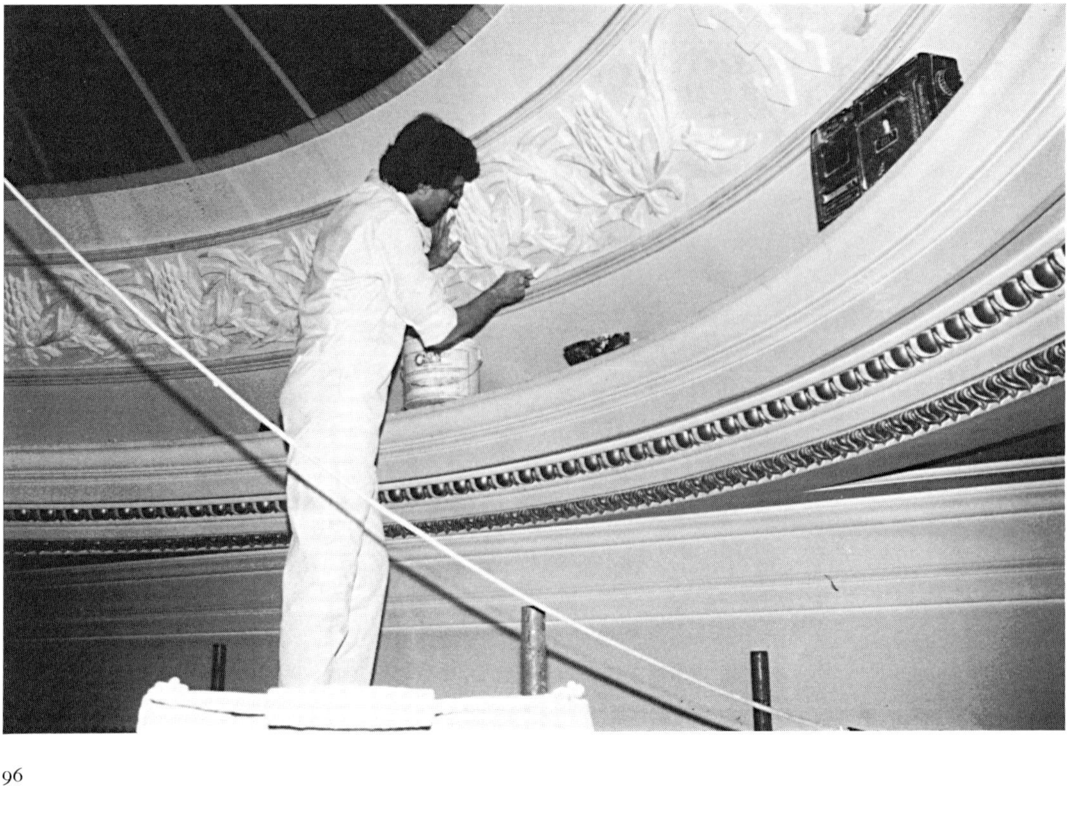

THE CEREMONIAL ROOMS

The staircase dome in 1983.

Forming the new plaster frieze to the dome. The design was based on existing panels above the doors in the Livery Hall.

Applying gold leaf to the architectural enrichments of the Grand Staircase landing.

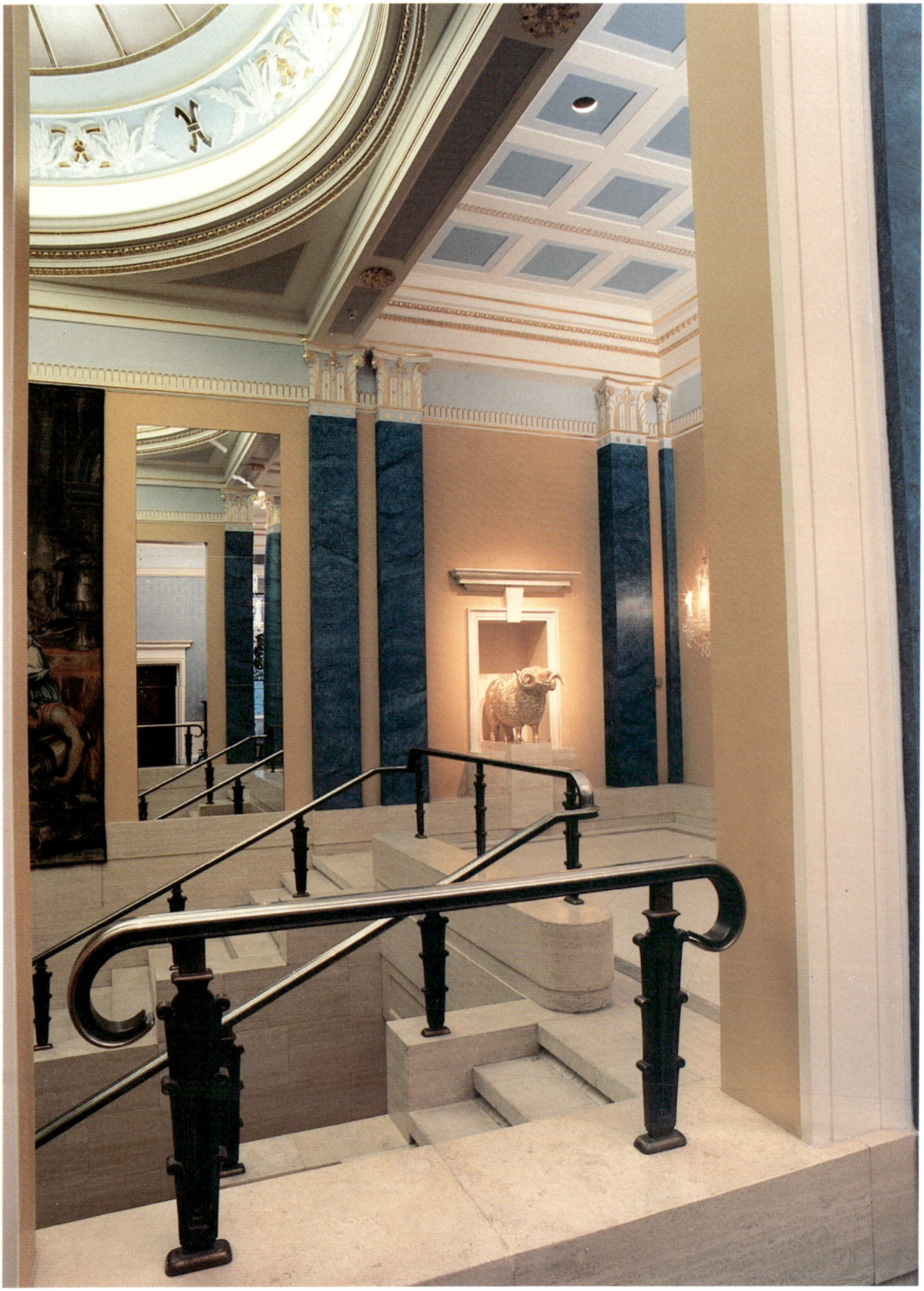

THE CEREMONIAL ROOMS

The Grand Staircase after refurbishment. At the top of the staircase stands the Company's Golden Ram in a newly-constructed niche of travertine marble.

View across the staircase towards the Reception Landing. The colour of the columns relates to those in the tapestries.

careful washing to revive this. The earlier scheme has now been extended, in matching $23\frac{1}{4}$ carat English gold leaf, to create a fuller and richer scheme.

Essentially part of the architectural experience of the staircase, but serving also as an ante-room to the Reception Room beyond, is the Reception Landing. It is linked with the staircase through a screen of columns and, to balance the sense of continuing space on this side of the stair, a panel of mirrored glass has been set into the blank north wall to create the illusion of a similar arrangement there.

THE CRAFTSMAN IN THE CITY

The new table on the half-landing of the Grand Staircase. The fretwork panel is made up of elements from the Livery Hall of the fourth Clothworkers' Hall and contains the cyphers of James I and Charles I.

THE CEREMONIAL ROOMS

The Reception Landing before refurbishment.

Alterations to the Reception Landing itself have been essentially cosmetic. A new dummy door has been built into the west wall to balance an existing one leading to the West Staircase, friezes and cornices have been provided above all the single doors, and a dado rail has been introduced. These additions have improved the proportions of the space and have given the west wall a balanced and symmetrical appearance when viewed through the doorway of the Reception Room.

The Landing and Reception Room have been decorated and furnished *en suite*, the walls of both being hung with blue silk and cotton damask, specially woven for Clothworkers' Hall by the Gainsborough Silk Weaving Company in Sudbury, Suffolk. The same fabric has been used for the curtains and upholstery. A deputation went to Sudbury

The Reception Landing after refurbishment. The new dummy door on the right balances the existing one leading to the West Staircase. The walls are hung in silk and cotton damask woven by The Gainsborough Silk Weaving Company.

The portrait of Sir William Stone, Master 1606–07, when James I was admitted to the Freedom of the Company, was purchased in 1984.

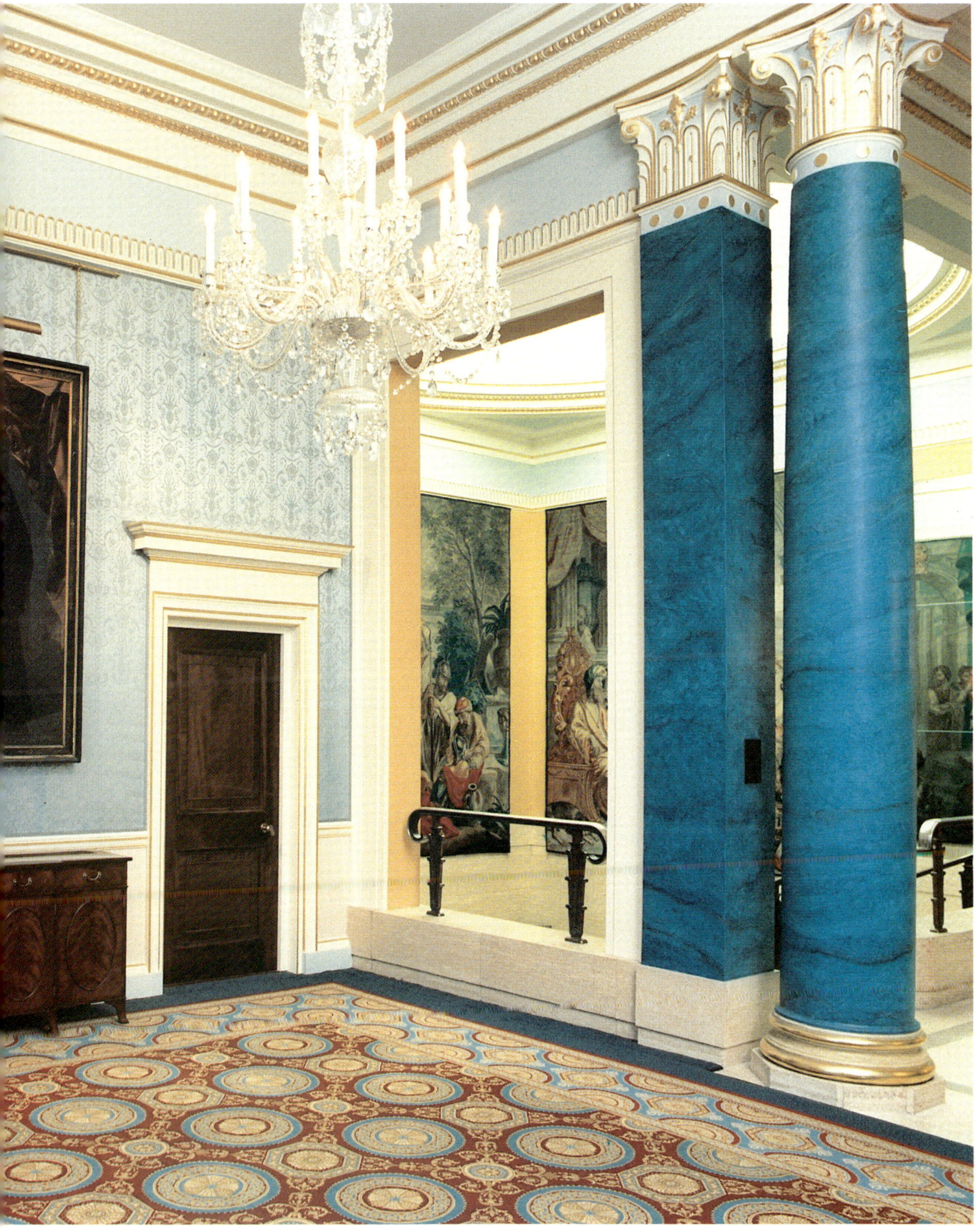

THE CRAFTSMAN IN THE CITY

Winding silk thread on to bobbins at the factory in Sudbury.

THE CEREMONIAL ROOMS

Gathering the silk from the bobbins on to a reed for transfer to the warping mill.

to watch the process of weaving: this time the Assistant Clerk and the author were accompanied by Peter Luttman-Johnson, past Master, and his wife. The silk thread is bought in hank from China. Over here it is sent away to be de-gummed and dyed before being returned in skeins to the factory. There each strand of silk is wound on to an individual bobbin; these are then mounted on a large frame called a creel, from which the threads can be drawn off in groups on to a reed ready for transfer to the warping mill. This is an extremely lengthy and painstaking operation, for across the warp of a four foot width of damask there are fourteen thousand and four hundred silk threads, and a creel can only take a maximum of four hundred bobbins at a time. Once the warping process is complete, the silk can be transferred from the mill drum

THE CRAFTSMAN IN THE CITY

The silk for the warp in place on the loom.

Winding the cotton from bobbins on to plugs for the weft.

to the warping beam at the back of the loom, and the individual threads drawn through the machine ready for the weft. The weft—that is the thread which runs across the warp—is cotton and is first transferred from bobbins on to plugs, which are in turn inserted in the shuttle that is pushed from side to side through the warp and causes the threads to be woven together. As in carpet-weaving, the pattern of the weave is controlled by a series of punched jacquard cards. The woven cloth comes off the loom

THE CEREMONIAL ROOMS

The plug in place in the shuttle and the woven damask as it emerges from the loom.

at the rate of between thirteen and sixteen yards a day; the Clothworkers' order was for four hundred and thirty yards.

A fine glass chandelier hangs from the ceiling of the Reception Landing and at the top of the Grand Staircase there is a matching pair of wall-brackets. These form part of a larger set made for the Hall by R. Wilkinson and Son. Apart from the drops, which come from Austria, they are English-made and English-built. The glass is cut in the nineteenth century manner, though the basic design derives from the age of Adam. The manufacture of a single glass canopy can be taken as a sample of the workmanship

THE CRAFTSMAN IN THE CITY

Mr Peter Luttman-Johnson discussing the process with the weaver.

Right: the damask being hung on the walls of the Reception Landing.

Following pages: building a chandelier at the workshops of R. Wilkinson and Son:
Cutting part of the central baluster of a chandelier on the carborundum wheel.
A baluster assembled.
Cutting a canopy for the top of the chandelier.
Stringing together the ropes of cut-glass buttons and drops.
One of a set of glass chandeliers and wall-brackets.

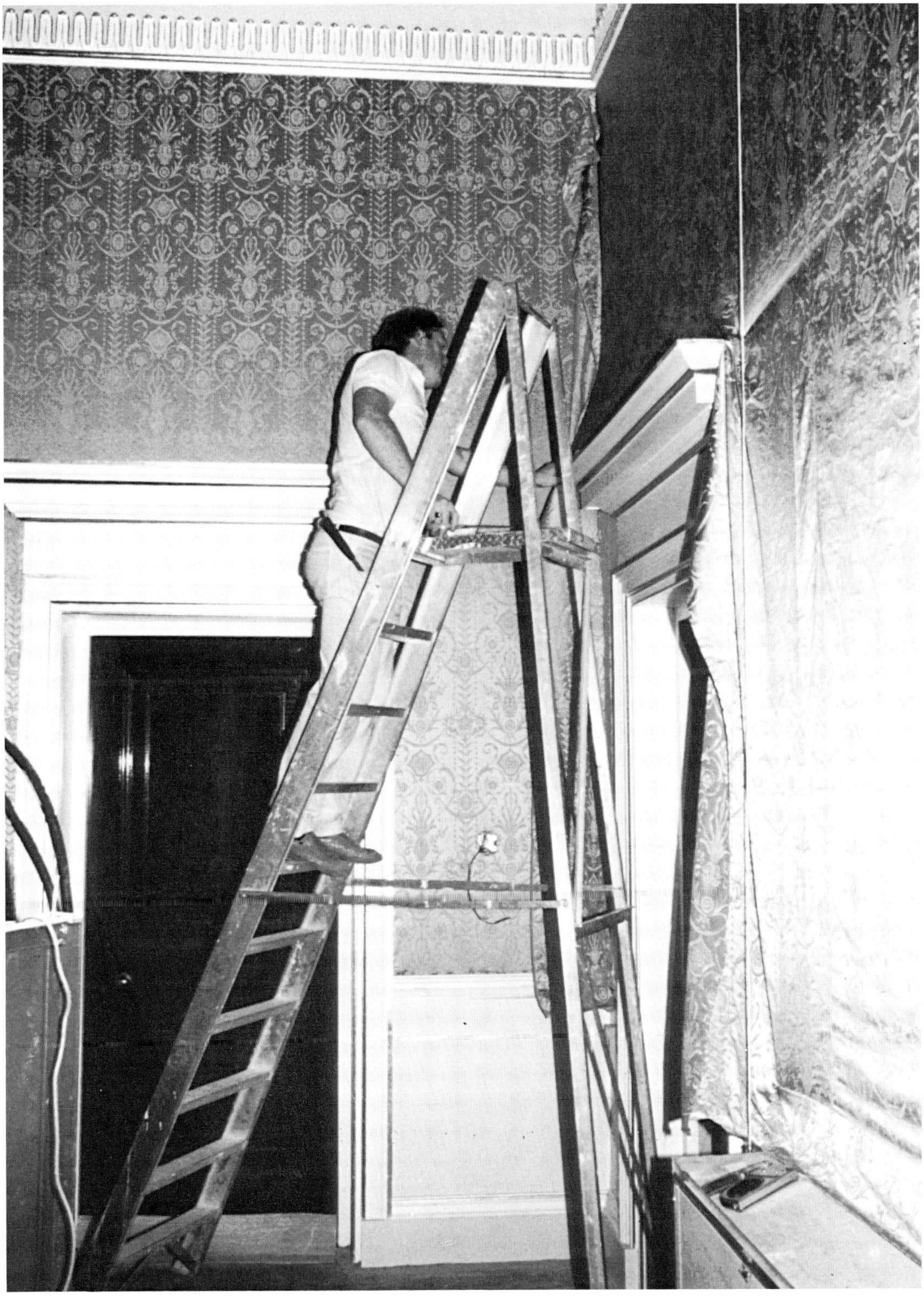

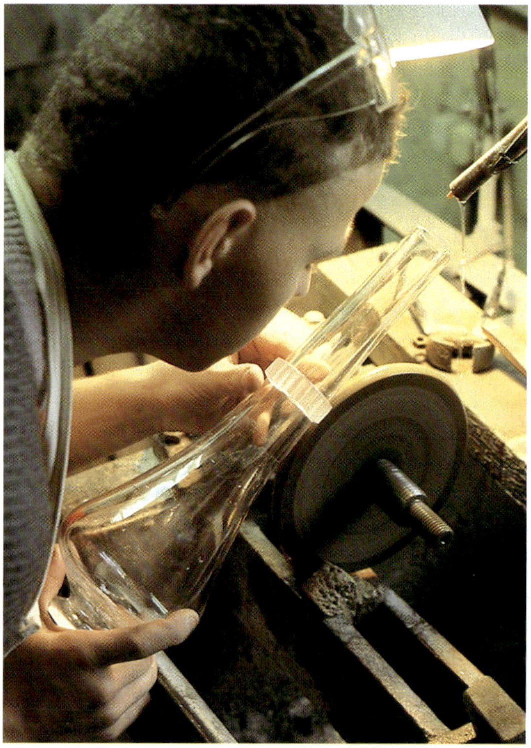

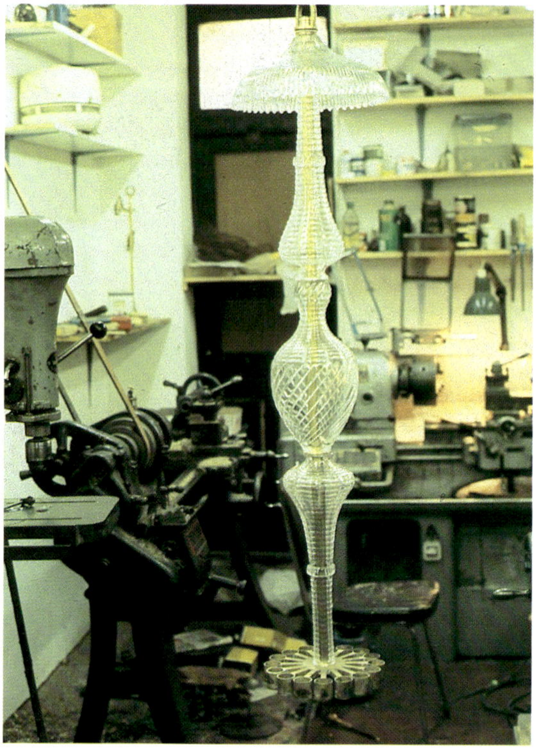

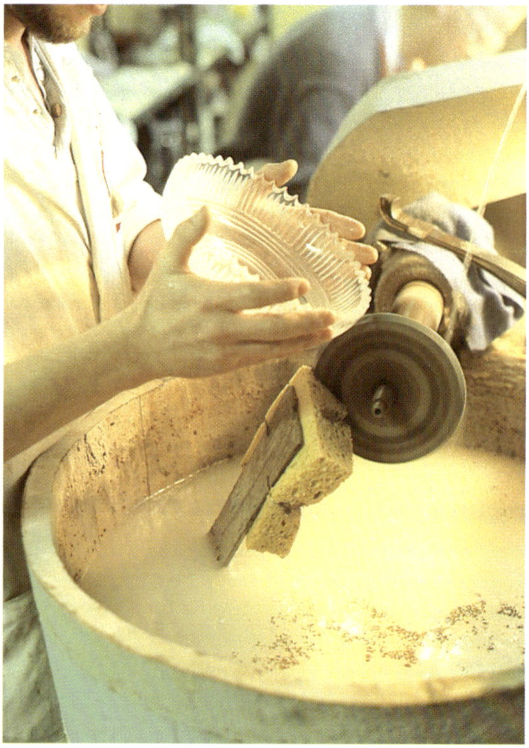

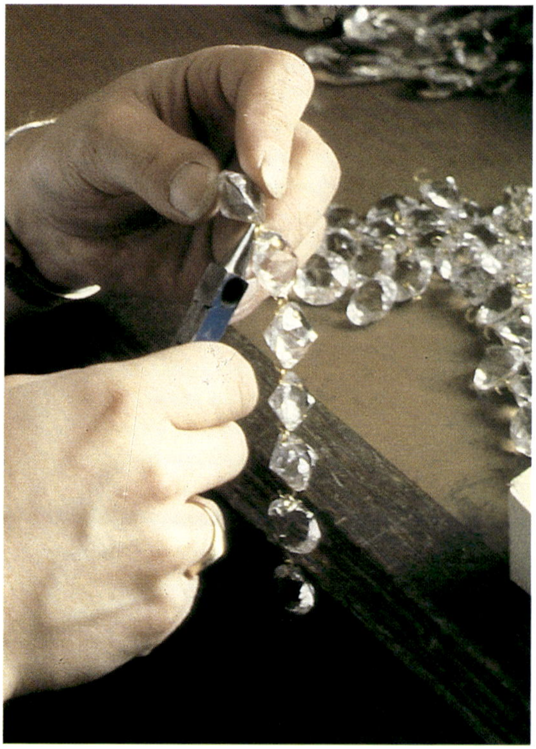

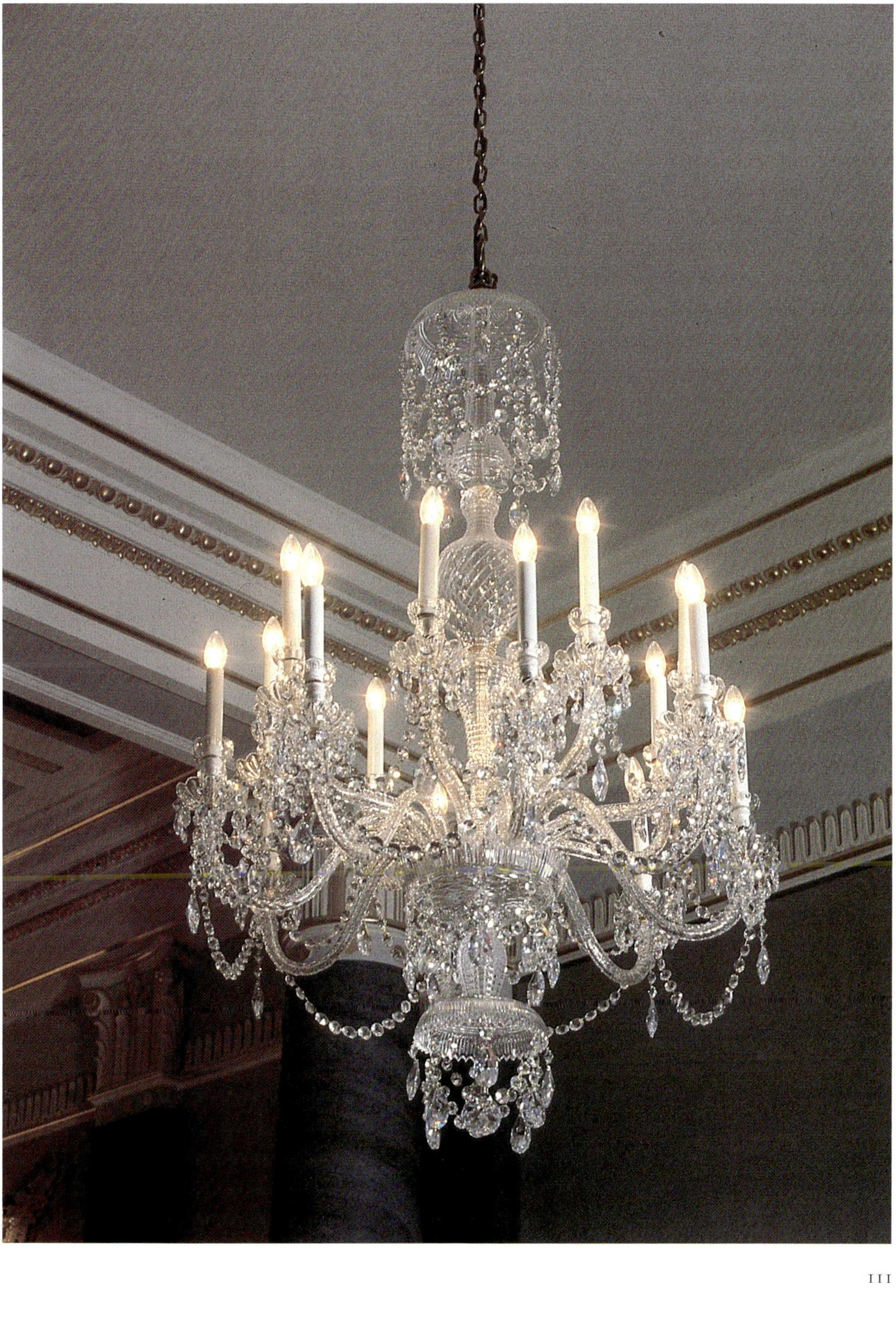

The Reception Room before refurbishment.

that goes into such a chandelier. The canopy starts as a blown bubble of clear glass, which is then halved, using a rotating diamond-coated saw. The half which is not to be cut is discarded; this is called the blow-over. After only the merest outline of the pattern has been marked on the glass, the first rough cuts are made on a carborundum wheel. These are then refined by the processes which follow. First is 'smoothing', using a natural stone wheel. Then come two stages of 'polishing', first with a mixture of pumice powder and water on a wood or cork wheel, then with a slurry of jeweller's rouge and water on a brush wheel. Once this has been washed off, the beauty of the newly-cut glass can be seen. The other parts—nozzles and pans to take the candle lights, and even the central stems which comprise three sections—are made in the same way. The pieces are linked together with a metal framework of hollow tubes for the electrical wiring. Where visible these are gilt; inside the glass they are silver-plated. Finally the chandelier is dressed with ropes of glass buttons and drops, each small piece of glass threaded to another by hand with tiny brass pins. The result is spectacular, especially when seen four at a time in the Reception Room.

The basic form of the Reception Room, as we have seen, follows that of the Drawing Room in the previous Hall; but although the ceilings are similar, unlike its prototype no decoration was provided in the 1950s at the ends of the room, in the spaces between the cornice and the curve of the vault. In the Victorian Hall, there had been a mural at one end depicting the story of Edward Osborne, who saved his master's daughter from drowning and rose from Clothworker apprentice to Lord Mayor of London. There was at one stage a move to reproduce this in the present room, but lack of sufficiently detailed evidence of the original, and the fact that there was no model for the other end of the room, resulted in the idea being abandoned. Instead these areas have now been decorated with plasterwork incorporating portrait medallions by John O'Connor depicting Samuel Pepys, Master 1677–78, and Thomas Massa Alsager, Master 1836–37, considered to be respectively the Company's most celebrated and most important Masters. The design is, like the rest of the room now, in the late-eighteenth century manner, the pairs of griffins with their arabesque tails being based on a design published by Thomas Sheraton in 1791. Such a motif seemed particularly appropriate to The Clothworkers' Company, whose coat of arms is supported by a pair of griffins. The new plaster griffins, like their heraldic counterparts which can be seen over the doors to the

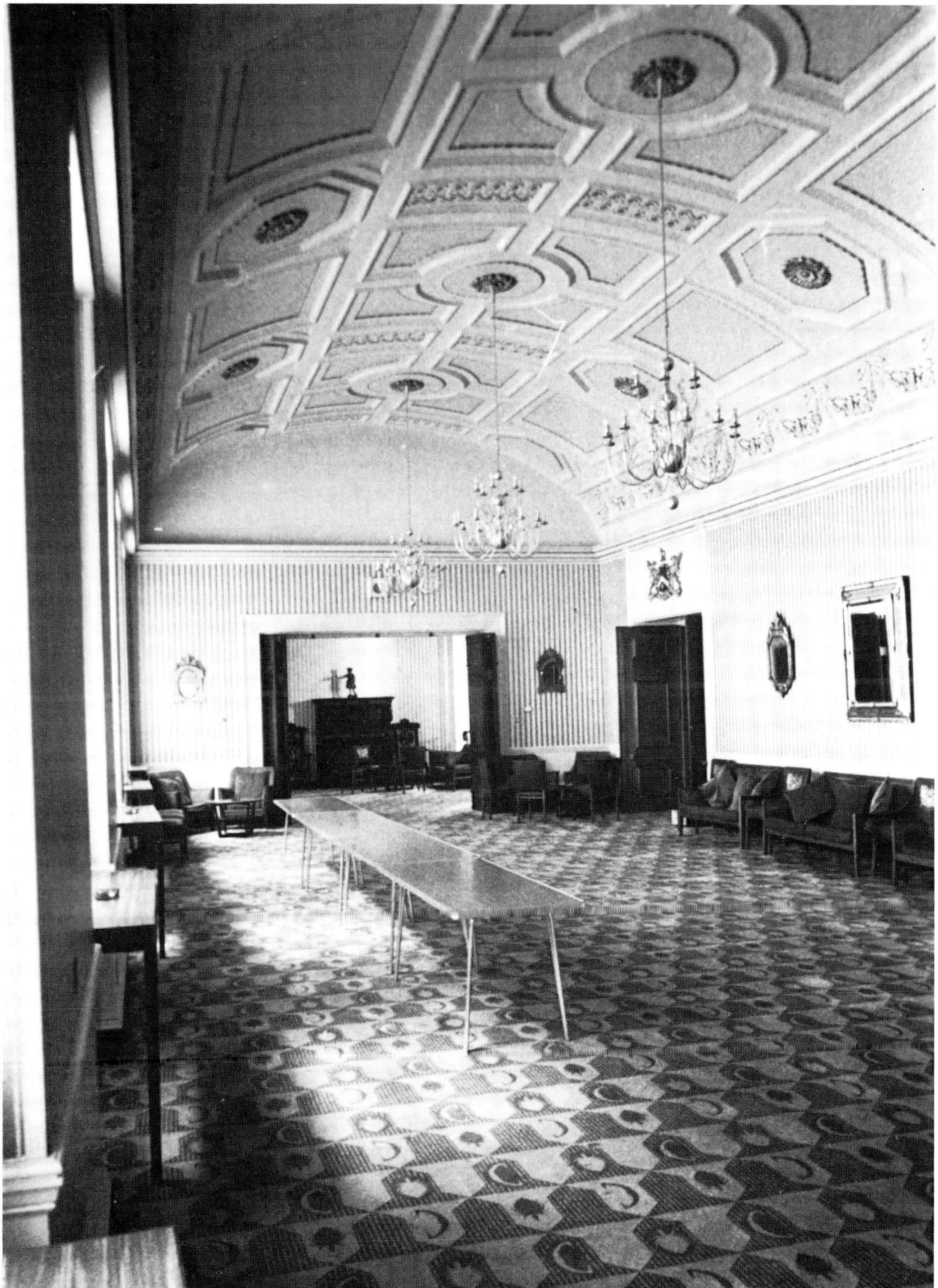

The Reception Room after refurbishment. It has been decorated and furnished *en suite* with the Reception Landing.

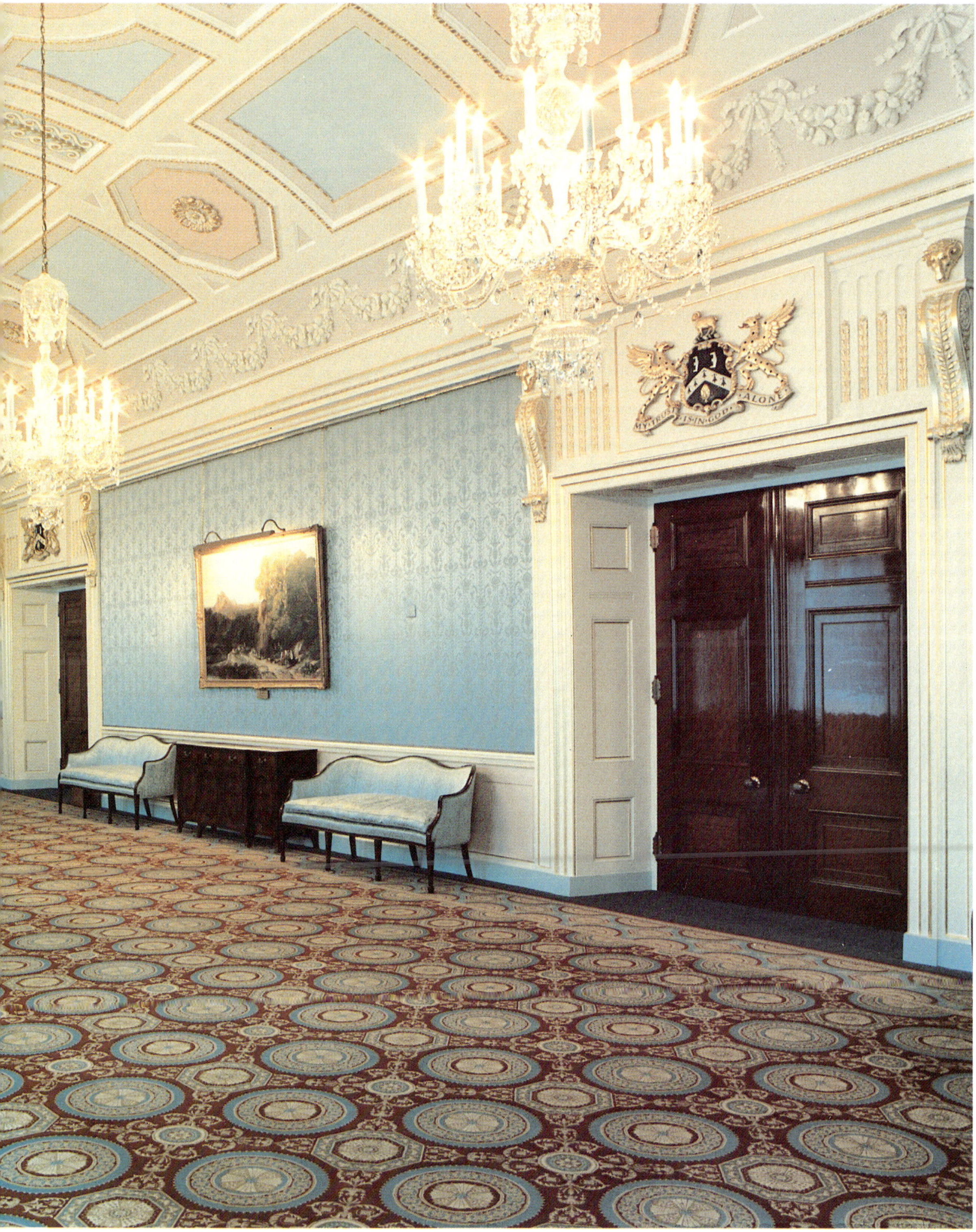
MY TRUST IS IN GOD ALONE

THE CRAFTSMAN IN THE CITY

Modelling a griffin in clay, from which were cast the moulds for the new plaster decoration in the Reception Room.

Livery Hall, are spotted. Clark and Fenn Ltd. carried out the plasterwork, returning to site some thirty years after constructing the ceiling of this room. The elements of the new design were first modelled in clay off site and, once approved, moulds were taken from them. These were then used for casting the plaster in sections, later to be

Sections of decorative plaster being fixed into place at the end of the Reception Room.

Following pages: plate published in 1791 from Thomas Sheraton's *The Cabinet-Maker and Upholsterer's Drawing-Book*.
New plaster decoration in the Reception Room, incorporating a medallion of Thomas Massa Alsager by John O'Connor.
One of the new doorcases in the Reception Room. Anthony Harrington's carvings enrich the joinery of Ashby and Horner.

brought to the Hall and put up piece by piece. Finally the whole composition was brought together by plastering the joins. The design was then complete, ready for painting and gilding: this was carried out by Clark and Fenn's painting section, which was responsible for all the decorations in both phases of the work.

More fine carving by Anthony Harrington is to be found in the Reception Room and in the Livery Hall. For much of the work in this phase he was acting as carving sub-contractor to Ashby and Horner. Their combined efforts with Harrington have produced two splendid new doorcases in the Reception Room. Harrington's carvings play an important role in providing the decorative embellishments for these pieces of joinery, but are also primary objects of great beauty in their own right. The form and detail of the pieces are in the Adam manner and the motifs of paterae, leaves and honeysuckle appear elsewhere in the room, in the silk damask and in the carpet. The ramsheads are doubly appropriate, for they were frequently used in neo-classical decora-

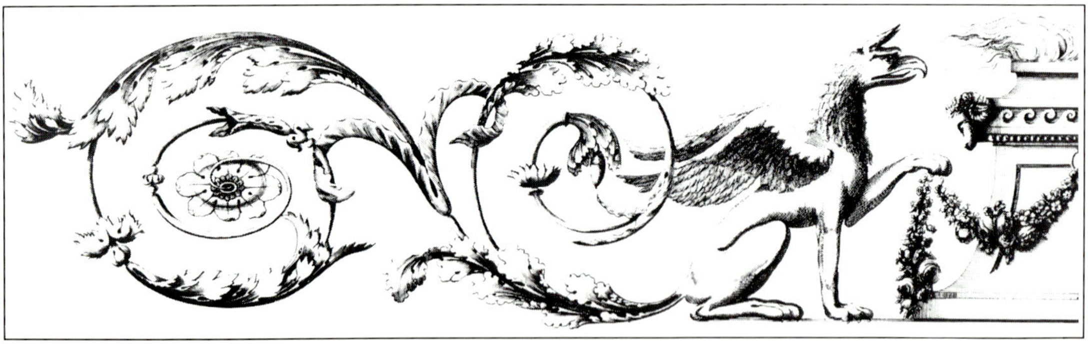

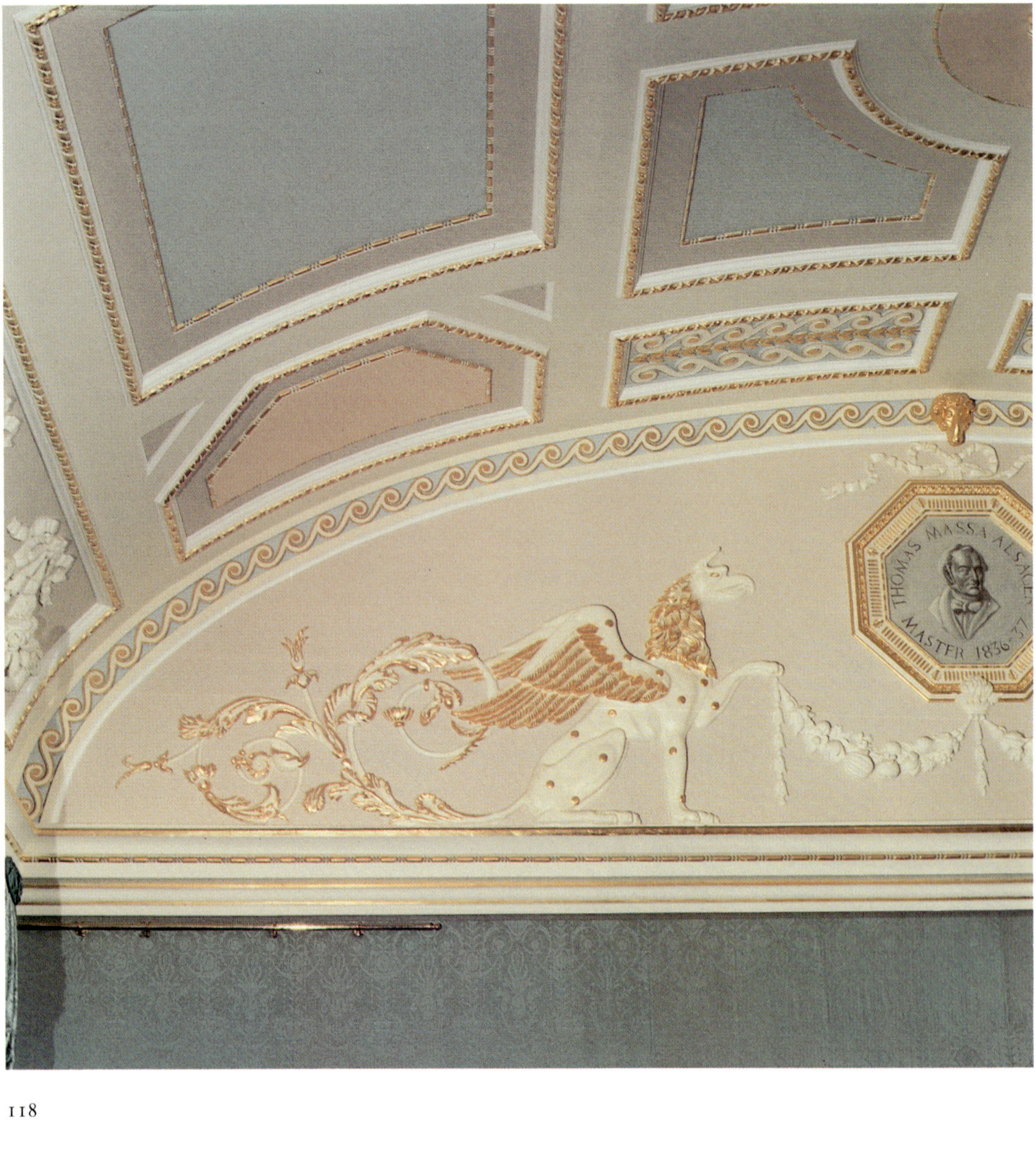
THOMAS MASSA ALSAGER
MASTER 1836-37

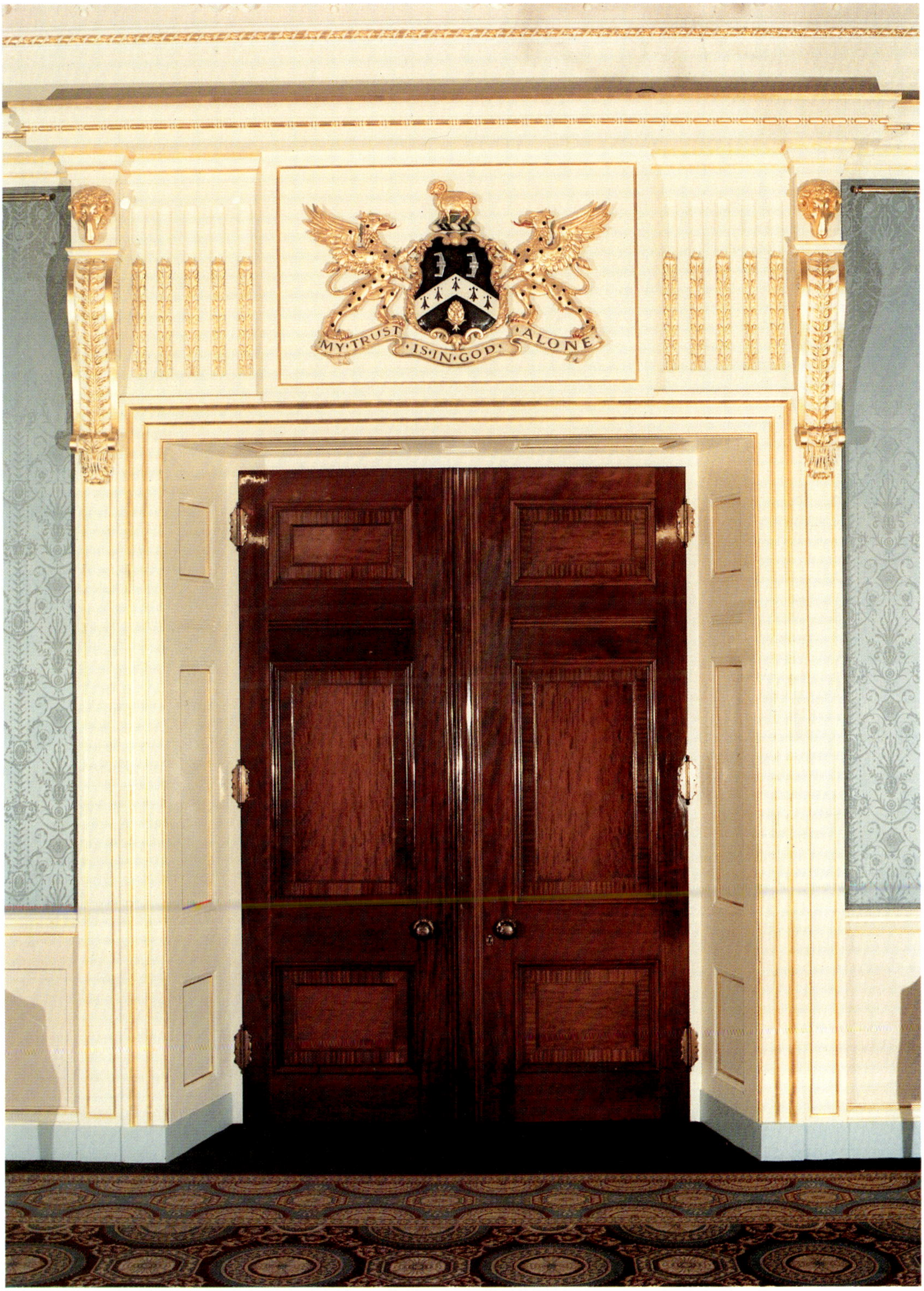
MY TRUST IS IN GOD ALONE

Anthony Harrington's carvings before incorporation in the works:
Details of the console brackets.
The ramsheads.

Opposite: the carvings painted and gilded on a doorcase in the Reception Room.

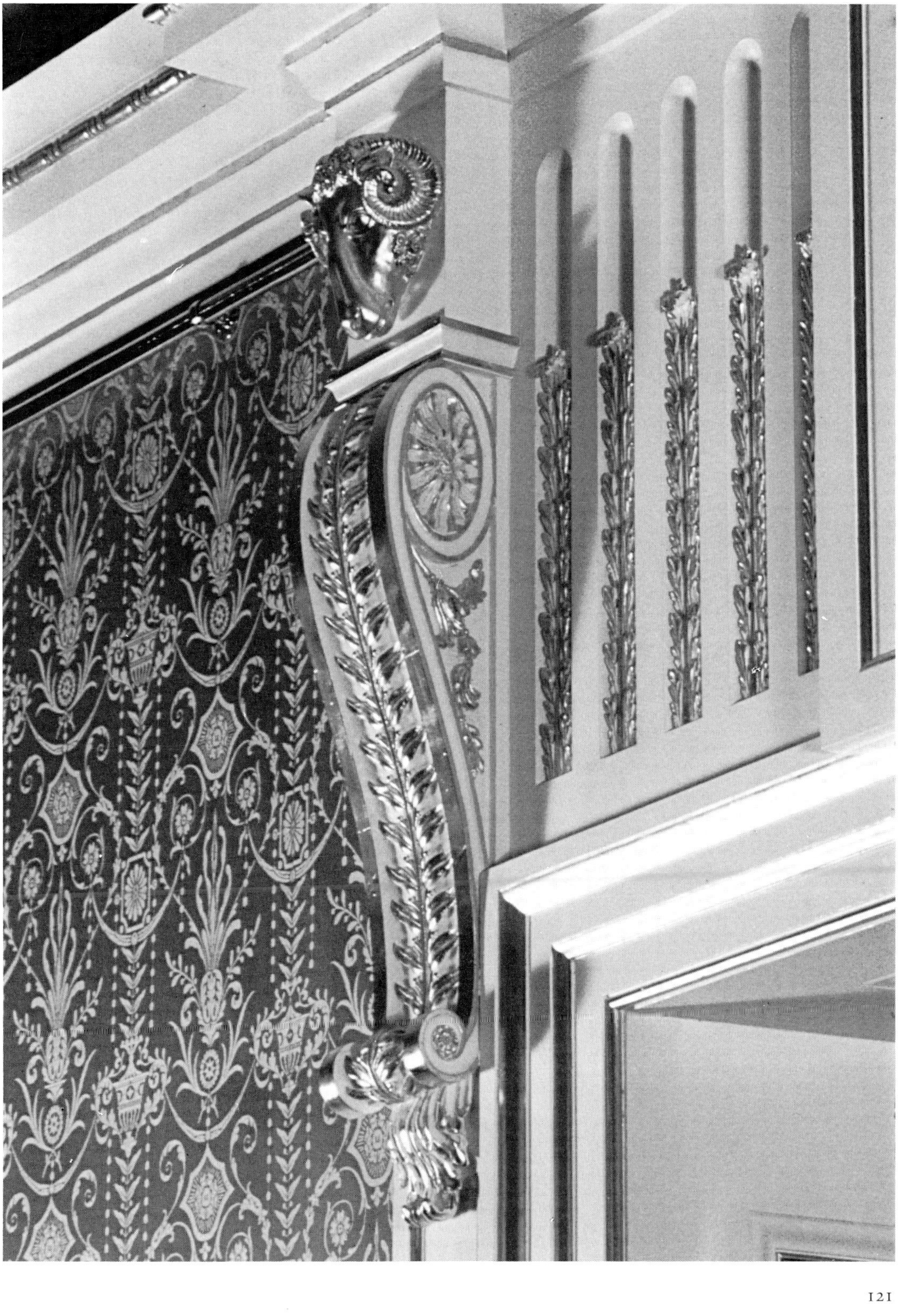

THE CRAFTSMAN IN THE CITY

A mock-up of one of the curtain valances at Charles Hammond's factory.

Above: the window wall of the Reception Room in 1983.

Below: the same view in 1987 after refurbishment.

tion and are of course of great significance for The Clothworkers' Company. Harrington also supplied the pier-glasses with carved and water-gilded frames; the plates of glass have been slightly distressed to reduce the hardness of the reflected image and to give a more mellow appearance.

Charles Hammond Ltd. made the curtains here and throughout the refurbished

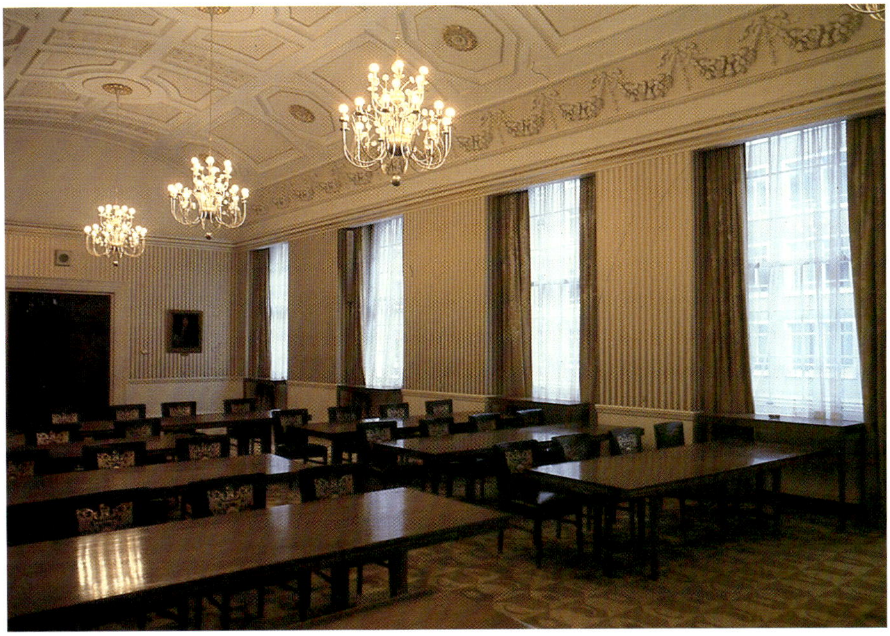

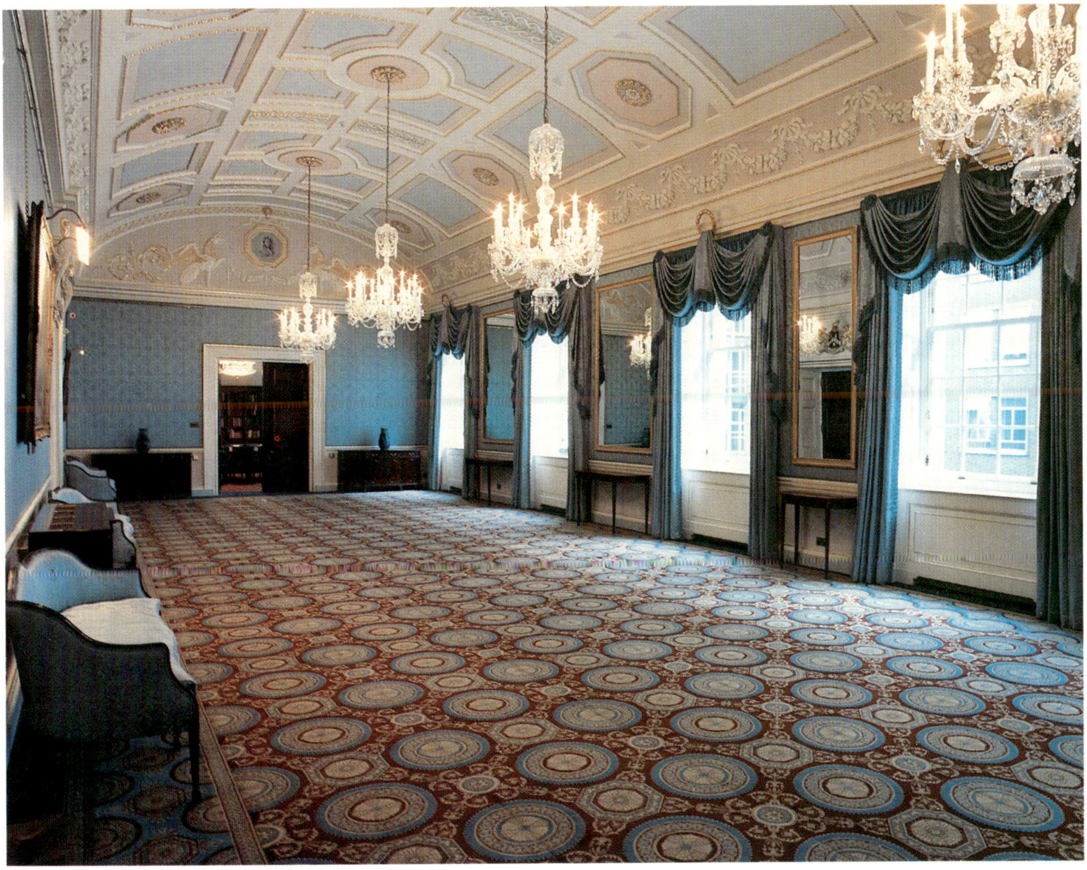

124

THE CEREMONIAL ROOMS

Above: a mahogany commode in Arthur Brett and Sons' workshop after veneering but before polishing.

Right and below: the commode in position at Clothworkers' Hall, showing how it is used to conceal a fan-coil unit.

A Hepplewhite-style sofa being upholstered in the workshop.

interiors. Those in the Reception Room are perhaps the grandest. The fringes and braids were made specially by C.J. Turner and Company (Trimmings) Ltd. in the City. Originally the curtains were hung behind the cornice in slots through which ventilation was supplied to the room. By modifying the ducts so that the air is now introduced through grilles just above the cornice, it has been possible to bring the curtains out on to the face of the wall and to provide richly swagged valances. These are gathered into carved and gilded laurel rings (by Harrington) which break the strong horizontal line of the cornice and give a greater sense of height to the windows.

The furniture, all of which is new and has been made for the room, comes from Arthur Brett and Son Ltd. in Norwich, supplied through Hammond Wholesale. The designs are based on pieces of the late-eighteenth century by Hepplewhite and Sheraton. The mahogany commodes with veneered oval panels are extremely functional: completely

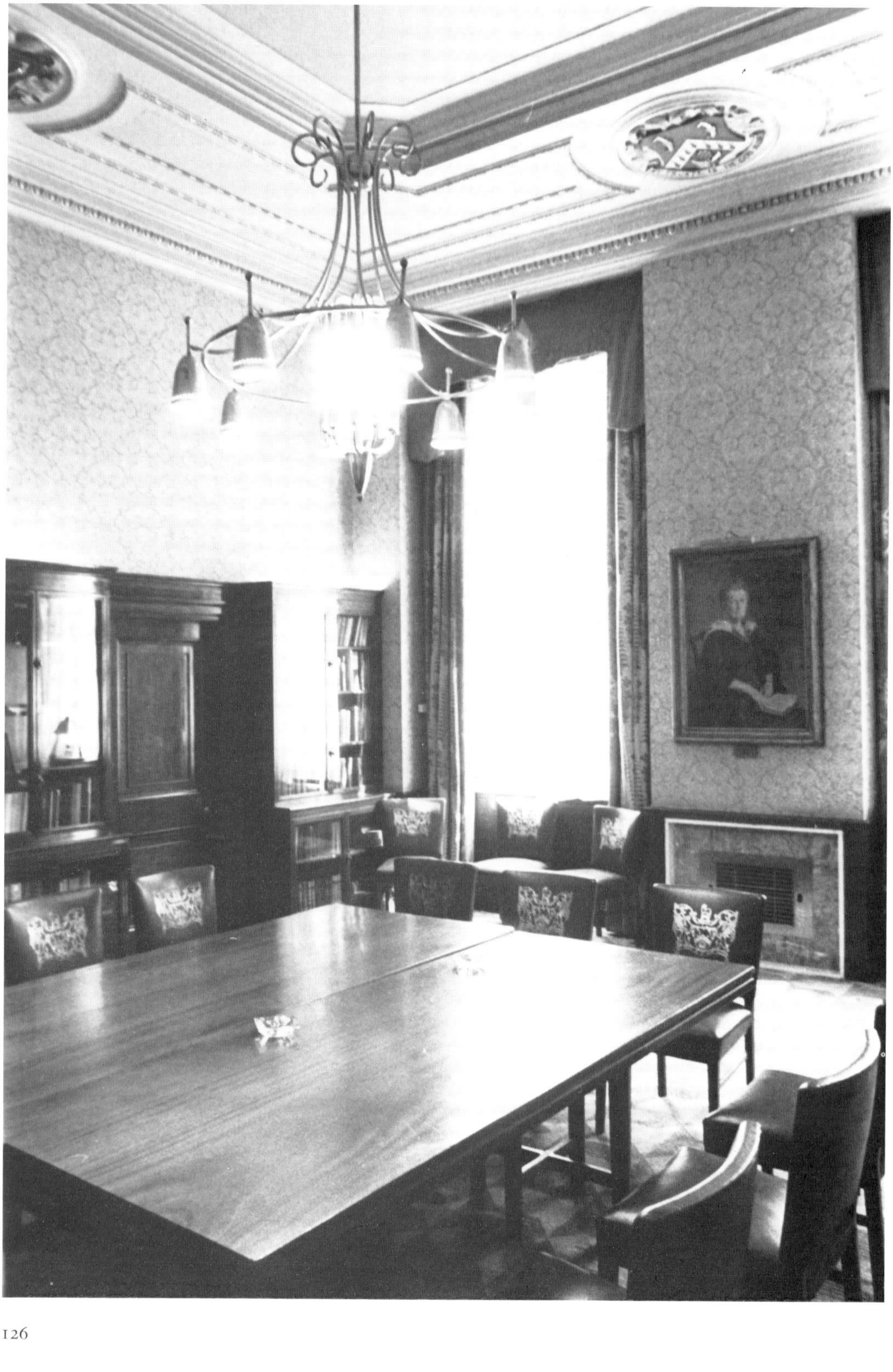

Opposite: the Library before refurbishment.

Right: Regency-style credenza by Arthur Brett and Sons in the Library.

Below: the Library after refurbishment. The original glazing to the bookcase doors has been replaced with elliptical brass grilles.

Above: the Livery Hall in 1983, looking north east towards the Gallery.

Below: architect's proposal for refurbishing the Livery Hall.

hollow, they serve to cover four of the fan-coil units installed to provide additional cooling. Five more units are concealed behind casings below the windows.

Brett's also made new furniture for the Library: a writing table and two Regency-style credenzas with tops of Belgian Fossil marble. They suit the early-nineteenth century mood of the room, as do the carpet and the curtains. The new linings to the windows are in mahogany to match the bookcases and existing joinery. The old softwood window frames and sashes have been 'grained' with paint to give the appearance of mahogany. To reduce the impact of the ventilation grilles in the room, a frieze and architrave have been added below the existing cornice and new grilles inserted within the depth of the frieze. Formerly the bookcase doors had been glazed with plate glass; this has now been replaced with elliptical brass grilles which allow the books to breathe and give a much richer appearance. The room is lit by a new cut-glass dish-light to the same design as those in the Court Room already described.

The climax of the building must surely be the Livery Hall, at once the largest space and ceremonially the most important. Unexecuted designs of the early 1950s indicate that it was originally intended to be rather richer. The design as built had a strongly horizontal, layered character, emphasised by the lighting from a string of wall-mounted up-lighters above the panelling. The unlined windows and corresponding recesses opposite were unbecomingly plain and, with no embellishments, missed the opportunity for providing a series of balancing vertical elements in the room. When viewed obliquely down the length of the Hall the many ventilation grilles set in the reveals were disturbingly prominent. Furthermore, the straight ends of the barrel-vaulted ceiling finished the room somewhat abruptly, reminding one of the 6th Duke of Devonshire's comment that being in his new state dining room at Chatsworth, which was of much the same form, was like sitting in a trunk waiting for someone to open the lid!

The principal changes effected by the refurbishment have sought to break up the horizontal lines of the room and to accentuate the vertical features. The intention has also been to enrich the interior to provide a setting appropriate to the formal and ceremonial occasions which take place here. Thus the old up-lighters have gone from the walls and two brass chandeliers now hang from the ceiling. These are supplemented by down-lighters recessed in the ceiling and a number of concealed spotlights directed on the pictures, the displays of plate and other decorative features. The windows and

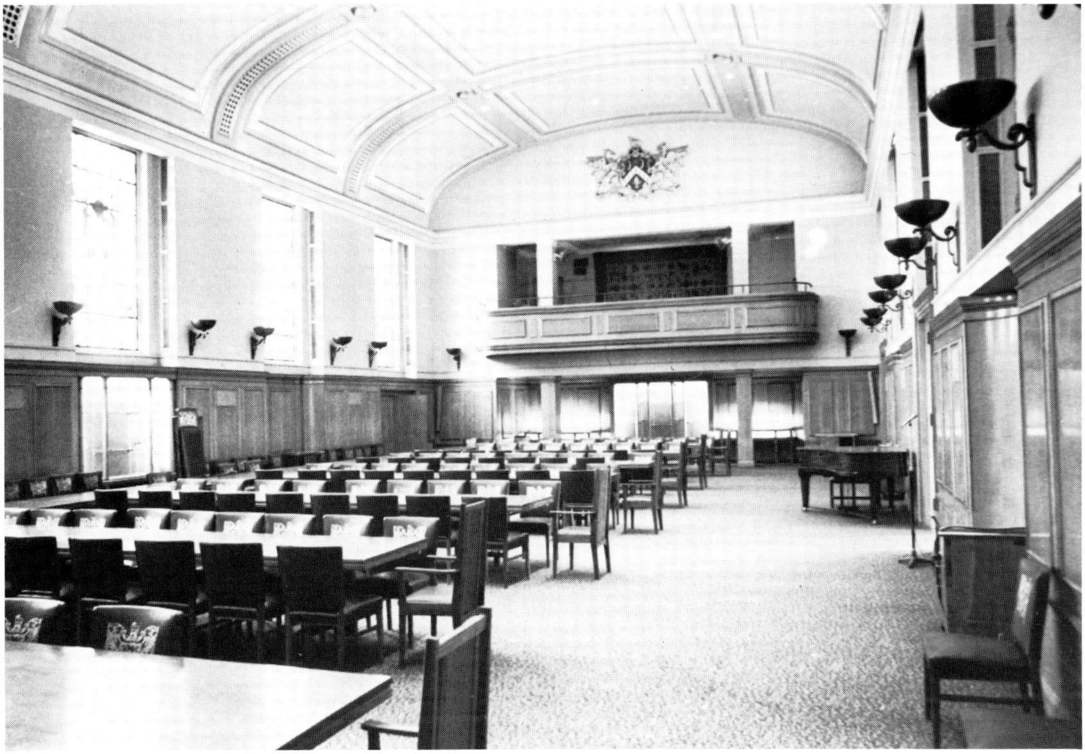

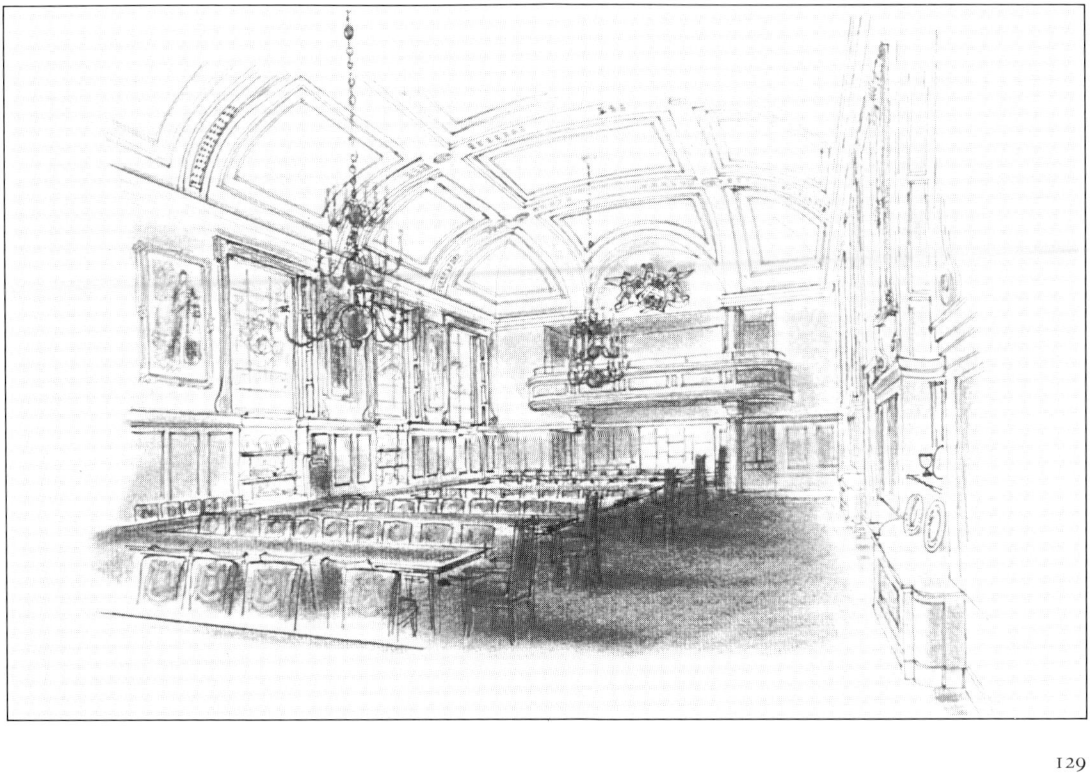

The Livery Hall after refurbishment, looking south east.

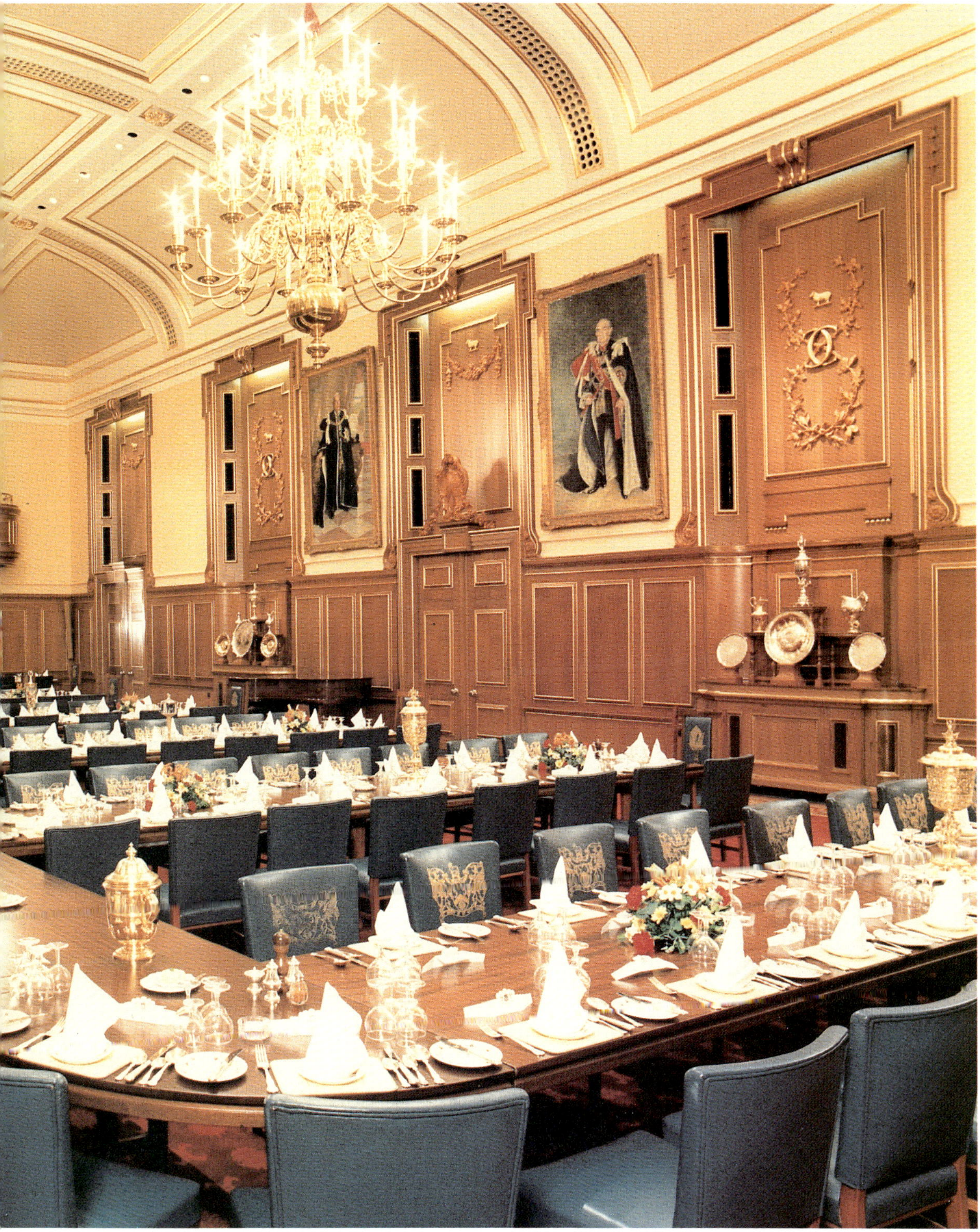

Above: forming the new hipped ends to the Livery Hall ceiling: the fibrous plaster ribs in place, with the metal lath awaiting the wet plaster.

Below: the plaster partially applied to the lath.

recesses have been lined in oak, embellished with carvings by Anthony Harrington. On the south wall, these take the place of the large portraits, which have now been brought out on to the wall-face between the windows and recesses. The ends of the vaulted ceiling have been hipped to produce a more contained and finished appearance, the vault at the east end being broken to contain the Company's coat of arms. The oak casings to the columns supporting the Gallery have been extended and new carved brackets provided to link them with the projecting balcony. The display of the Company's plate has been brought out from under the Gallery and located more prominently in the body of the Hall on five oak buffets, which also contain plate-warming cupboards and conceal five of the thirteen fan-coil units now installed to provide additional environmental control. The colour of the panelling is slightly darker and richer than before and the mouldings have been highlighted in gold leaf. Finally the public address system has been upgraded, with an induction loop provided for those with hearing aids, and a system of television monitors installed to protect the Company's plate when it is on show.

The process of hipping the ceiling was tackled by Classical Plasterers Ltd. from West Yorkshire. The old ceiling had been constructed as a huge shell of fibrous plaster suspended on metal straps and bars from the flat concrete slab and beams which form the roof above the Livery Hall. To achieve the required affect, the end bays of the old ceiling were cut out and replaced with new sections in the desired form; the three central bays remained untouched. Scale models, first in card and then to a larger scale in plaster, enabled the geometry to be worked out. Because of the restricted programme, the new parts have been constructed differently from the old. Only the main ribs which define the line of the new form are in fibrous plaster; the panels between have been formed in metal lath and then plastered wet on site. After drying, a final sprayed coat of acoustically absorbent plaster was applied as a finish both to the new work and to the existing ceiling where the old hair-mat acoustic linings had been stripped off.

The need for a considerable scaffold which filled the Hall meant that all this work had to be completed as soon as possible. Even the decorations had to be finished before any joinery work could be started in the rest of the room; and only when the scaffold had gone, could the alterations and additions to the panelling be made. When this did happen, it happened very fast, because Ashby and Horner had been busy preparing the

133

The Livery Hall during the works. The ceiling has been completed and joinery is being fixed from movable towers.

Below: one of the recesses along the south wall in 1983.

Right: the same recess lined in oak and enriched with carvings. The buffet is one of five on which the Company plate is now displayed. Inside are fan-coil units and hot cupboards for warming plates.

> Sewing sections of the great carpet together.
>
> Elements of the two brass chandeliers waiting to be lacquered at Dernier and Hamlyn's works.
>
> The Livery Hall carpet. The body has a repeated pattern of habicks and teasels; teasels also appear in the border.
>
> *Following pages*: the Court and Livery Dinner on 10 December 1986.

new work off site in their Essex workshops. Only the final fitting and polishing were carried out on site, the latter being necessarily a site process to ensure consistency. Once the joinery was in place, the new carved enrichments could be brought to the site. For the Livery Hall, these were in the manner of Grinling Gibbons, consistent with the Wren-like character of the room. For the recesses above the doors there were swags of fruit and flowers all carved in lime, and for the recesses above the buffets in between, entwined branches of oak and laurel, incorporating crossed 'C's and gilded rams. Small carvings of bell-flower drops and scrolls in oak now enrich the architraves to all the recesses and windows, and above the central door from the Reception Room stands a splendid cartouche in lime bearing the Company's coat of arms, draped with swags of fruit, flowers and teasels.

With the high level work in place and the bulk of the scaffold towers cleared away, the lonely process of sewing together the huge carpet could begin. Unlike in the smaller rooms, where the carpets arrived in one piece, the Livery Hall carpet is so large that it had to be delivered in sections and hand-sewn together on site. It is a splendid carpet and a completely original design. The body, in two tones of red, has a repeated pattern of habicks and teasels; in the richly-coloured border more teasels are interwoven with foliage and flowers. The great rectangle defined by the border is set within a deep blue margin, which links together the carpets in all the rooms on this floor, running through doorways, under the Gallery and into window recesses.

Finally the Livery Hall chandeliers: two thirty-six branch brass fittings of traditional Flemish design hang from new plaster roses set on the centre-line of the high vaulted ceiling. They were made in south London by Dernier and Hamlyn Ltd. who, it was discovered at the end of the job, had made many of the light-fittings for the Hall in the 1950s. Each chandelier left the factory as hundreds of individual cast, spun and extruded brass elements to be systematically assembled on site. They were one of the last items to arrive for, in order that the chandeliers should not appear too bright and new, it had been decided to let the brass tarnish slightly before coating it with lacquer. The process took surprisingly long.

Once the chandeliers had been assembled and winched into place, the Livery Hall tables and chairs could be returned to their home. All was now in readiness for the important deadline of the first Court and Livery Dinner on 10 December 1986. The

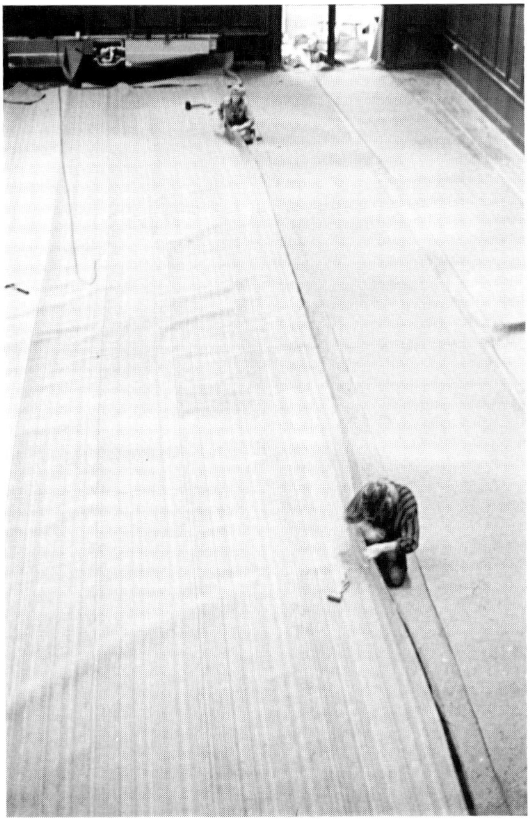

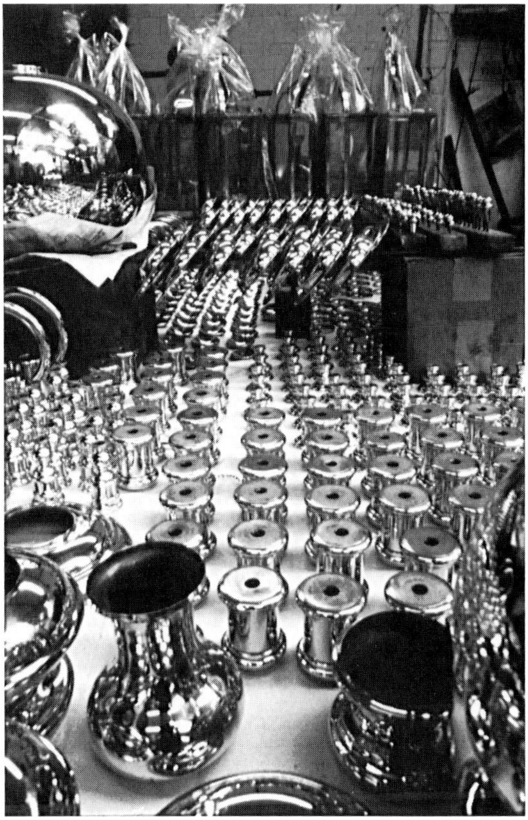

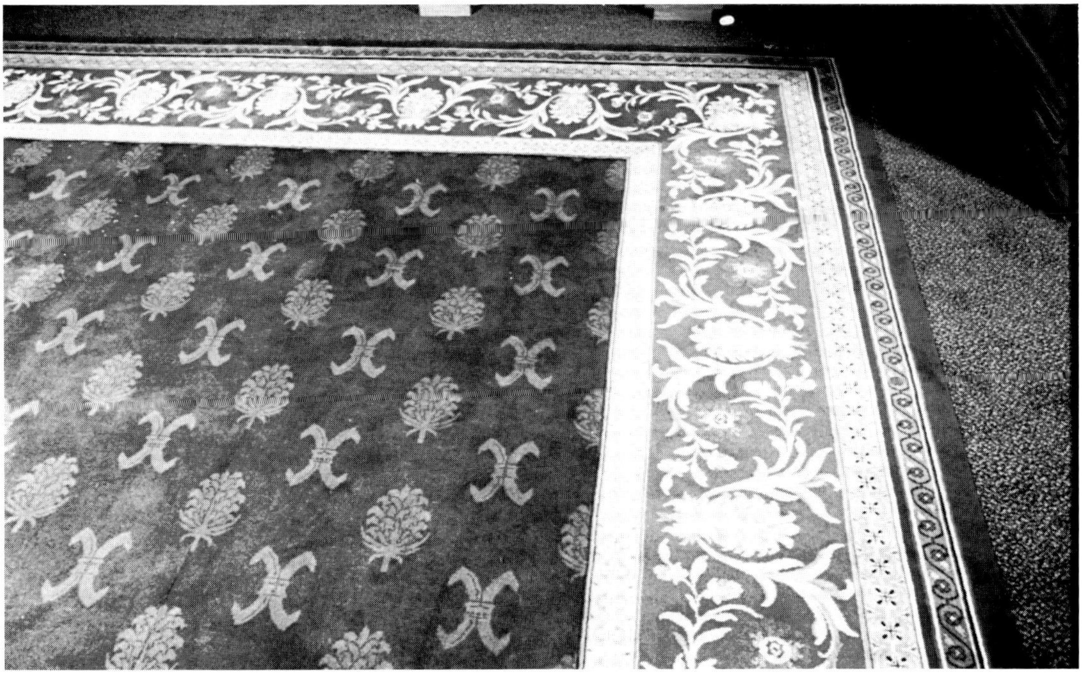

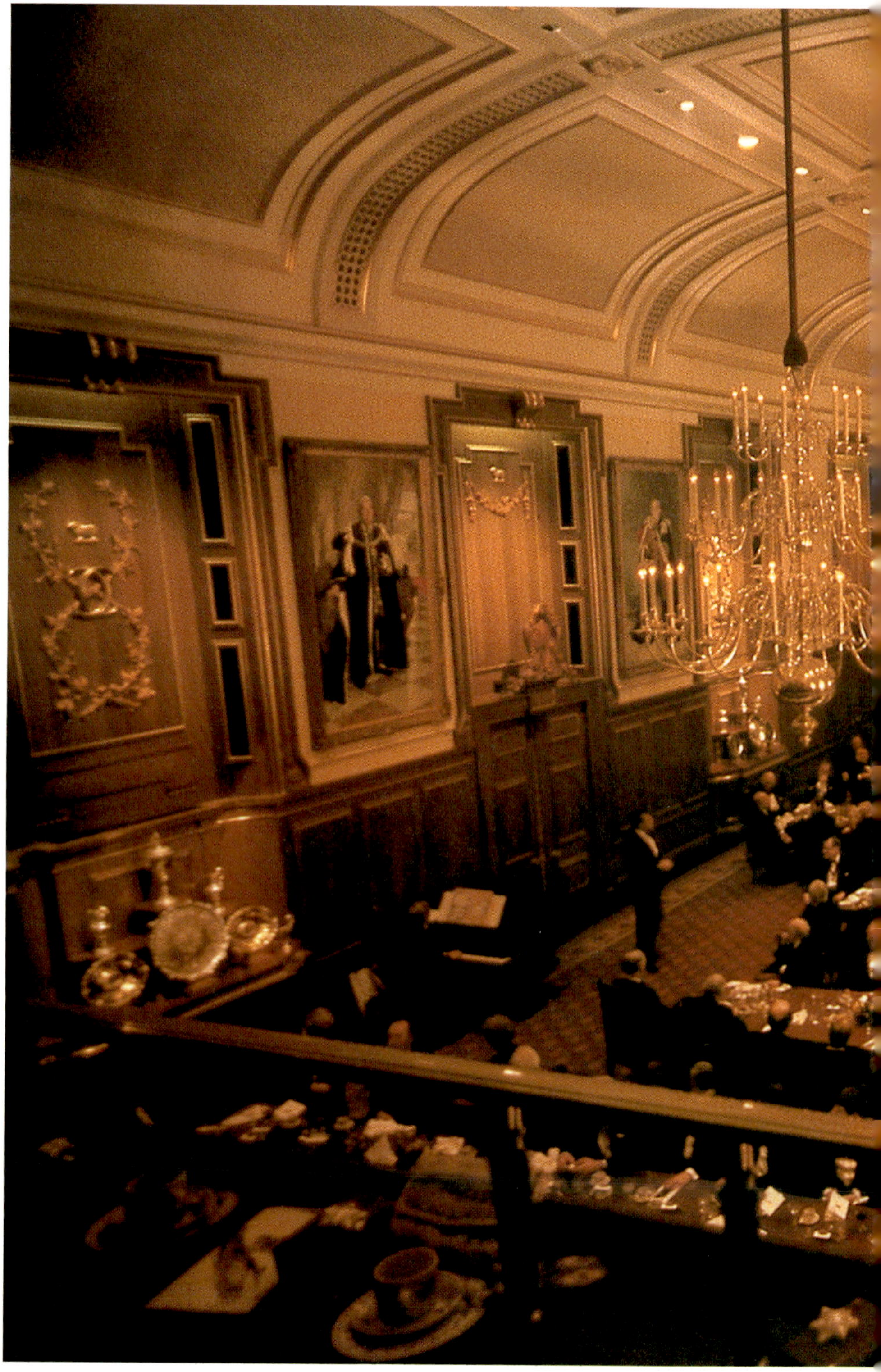

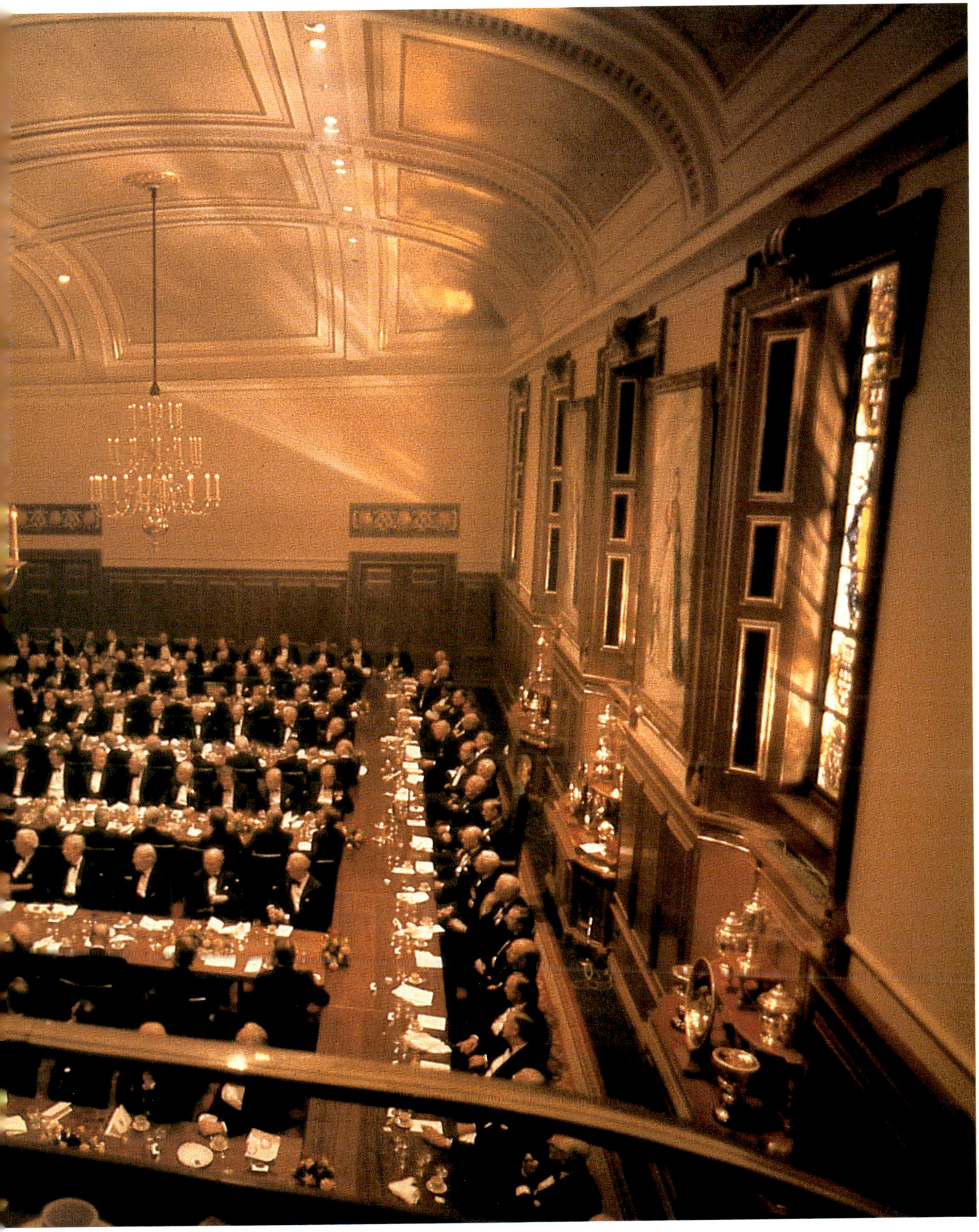

project had been completed to the highest standards, within budget and on time, demonstrating the effectiveness of careful planning and co-ordination, and the skill and commitment of British craftsmen and women, when called on to give of their best.

On 17 July 1987, the Lord Mayor of London, the Rt. Hon. Sir David Rowe-Ham GBE, visited Clothworkers' Hall to present the City Heritage Award 1987, which recognised the project as the best example of building conservation completed in the City of London in 1986. This splendid occasion served as a gratifying epilogue to the endeavours of all those concerned. The climax, however, must surely have been on the night of 10 December, when once more the Company's magnificent plate was brought out, its members gathered in the refurbished Hall and a new chapter in the long history of The Clothworkers' Company was heralded by the traditional toast:

> Prosperity to The Clothworkers' Company,
> Root and Branch, and may it flourish
> for ever!

THE CEREMONIAL ROOMS

The coat of arms of The Clothworkers' Company: carved in stone for the fifth Hall, it is now incorporated above the entrance to the present Hall.

ACKNOWLEDGEMENTS

CLOTHWORKERS' HALL REFURBISHMENT 1985/86

Consultants
Project Managers: Richard Ellis
Architects: Donald W. Insall and Associates Ltd
Consulting Services Engineers: Sir Frederick Snow and Partners
Consulting Structural Engineers: Andrews, Kent and Stone
Quantity Surveyors: Gardiner and Theobald
Acoustic Consultants: Sound Research Laboratories Ltd
Security Consultants: Defence Systems Ltd

Management Contractor
Higgs and Hill Management Contracting Ltd

Sub-contractors
General builder's work: T. A. Martin and Sons Ltd
Asbestos removal: Cape Contracts Ltd (*Stage 1*), Kitsons Environmental Systems Ltd (*Stage 2*)
Asphalt work: Porchland Asphalt Ltd
Lift refurbishment: Hammond and Champness Ltd (*Stage 1*), Otis Elevator PLC (*Stage 2*)
Mechanical and electrical installations: Longstaff and Shaw Ltd (*Stage 1*), Matthew Hall Ltd (*Stage 2*)
Plumbing and drainage: Baker & Freeman Ltd
Joinery: Elliotts of Reading (*Stage 1*), Ashby and Horner Joinery Ltd (*Stage 2*)
Plasterwork: Classical Plasterers Ltd, Clark and Fenn Ltd
Tiling: Wingrove Tiling Ltd (*Stage 1*), Parkinson (Wall Tiling) Ltd (*Stage 2*)
Carpet fitting: Albany Carpets Ltd
Linoleum and vinyl flooring: Variety Floors Ltd
Suspended ceilings: Roskel Contracts Ltd
Painting and decoration: Clark and Fenn Ltd
Boiler flues: Chimney Maintenance Services (London) Ltd
Archive store shelving: Libraco Ltd
Sanitary fittings: Folkard Bolding Ltd (*Stage 1*), Higgs and Hill Building Ltd (*Stage 2*)
Terrazzo flooring: Fieldmount (Terrazzo) Ltd
Dry-lining and stud partitions: Hill Bros (Uxbridge) Ltd
Marble and stonework: Albion Stone Masonry Ltd

ACKNOWLEDGEMENTS

Metalwork: Qualart Ltd
Bronze and glass doors: Pollards of London Ltd
Stained glass cleaning and repairs: The Glass House
Security shutters: Continental Shutters Ltd
Damask Walling: Charles Hammond Ltd

Specialist Suppliers
Silk and cotton damask: The Gainsborough Silk Weaving Company Ltd
Soft furnishings: Charles Hammond Ltd
Curtain trimmings: A. Sindall Ltd, G. J. Turner and Co (Trimmings) Ltd
Curtain poles and finials: Tempus Stet Ltd
Leather upholstery: Connolly Bros (Curriers) Ltd
Carpets: Woodward Grosvenor and Co Ltd
Wallpapers: Cole and Son (Wallpapers) Ltd, Osborne and Little PLC, Zoffany Ltd, Tectura Ltd, Helen Sheane Wallcoverings Ltd
Murals: Susan Llewellyn Associates (Artist: John O'Connor)
Carvings: Anthony Harrington
Drawing Room chimneypiece: Crowther of Syon Lodge Ltd
Architectural ironmongery: Yannedis and Co Ltd
Brass bookcase grilles: J. D. Beardmore and Co Ltd
Coat-hanging systems: A. J. Binns Ltd
Furniture: Hammond Wholesale (Arthur Brett and Sons Ltd), Elliotts of Reading, Ashby and Horner Joinery Ltd, R. Tyzack Ltd, Browns of West Wycombe, Martin Dodge (Interiors) Ltd, L. M. Kingcome Ltd, Wooltons Ltd, The Cotswold Furniture Company, Ergonom Ltd
Picure framing: The Addison-Ross Gallery
Chandeliers, lanterns and lamps: R. Wilkinson and Sons, Dernier and Hamlyn Ltd, David Paton (London) Ltd, W. Sitch and Co Ltd, R. J. Chelsom and Company Ltd Christopher Wray Lighting Emporium, Clare House Ltd, Mr. Light, Arnold Montrose Ltd
Display Lighting: Light Graphix Ltd, Raxcrest Electrical Ltd
Security cameras: Chubb Alarms Ltd
Public address installation: Philips Communications and Security
Electrical accessories: Hamilton Litestat
Catering equipment: Stott Benham Ltd, Stangard Metal Workers Ltd
Acoustic panels: Applied Acoustics – Venables Ltd
Signs: Rivermeade Signs Ltd, Burnham and Co (Onyx) Ltd
Mirrors: The Sander Mirror Company Ltd
Kitchen roofing system: H. H. Robertson (UK) Ltd